MW01700157

THE INVALIDES

THE ARMY MUSEUM - THE TOMB OF NAPOLEON

art lys

Musée de l'Armée Invalides

Author: Boris Bouget (Army Museum, Division of Historical Research, Educational Initiatives and Mediation or DRHAPM)

We would like to express our deepest gratitude to General Christian Baptiste and David Guillet, director and deputy director of the Army Museum, as well as Philippe de Bernard, Christophe Bertrand, Émilie Cambier, Bertrand Campeis, Agathe Formery, Stéphanie Froger, Jordan Gaspin, Jean-François Gaudin, Charlotte Georges-Picot, Vincent Giraudier, Valérie Godard, Christine Helfrich, Carine Lachèvre, François Lagrange, Olivia Laurent, Antoine Leduc, Sylvie Leluc, Sylvie Le Ray-Burimi, Anne-Sylvaine Marre-Noël, Prune Paycha, Sylvie Picolet, Christophe Pommier, Olivier Renaudeau, Émilie Robbe, Béatrice Six, Grégory Spourdos and Julien Voinot, while not forgetting François Soffer (the Army Museum's Society of Friends).

Contents

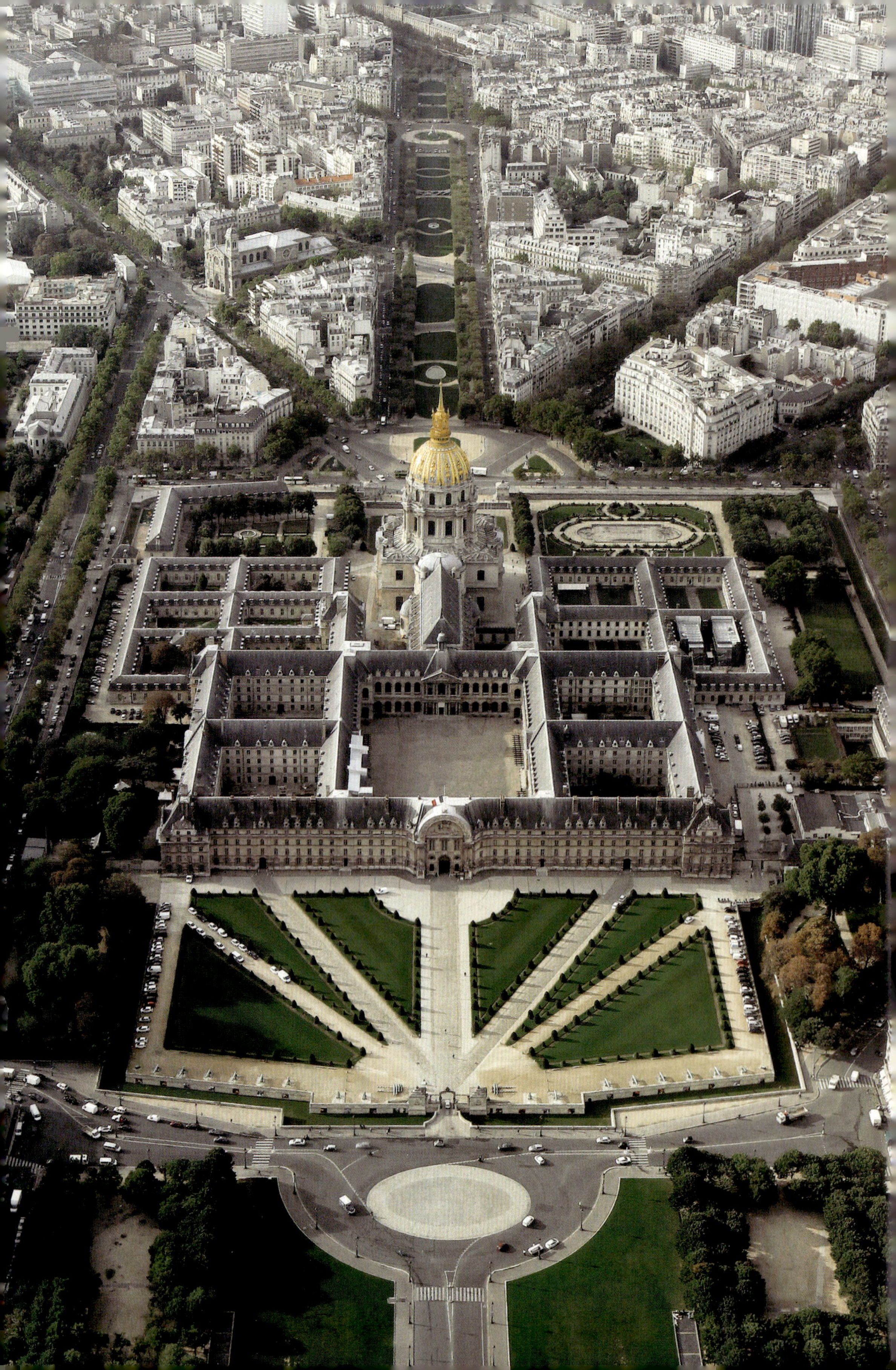

The Hôtel National des Invalides is a major Parisian edifice. Not only is it one of the city's largest and most impressive buildings but it is also one of the few that has lost none of its coherence and stylistic unity.
More than four million visitors walk through its gates each year, attracted by its reputation, the silhouette of the Dome against the capital's skyline, the tomb of Napoleon and the masterpieces in the Army Museum's collections.
Yet many leave without fully discovering its wealth of detail and extraordinary diversity. On its own, the «promenade» of the spectacular cannons overlooking the moats and bordering the courtyard takes half a day for the many people who embark on it.
The same is true for exploring the Cathedral and the Dome with their carved and painted decorative features. Not to mention a walk through the galleries, evoking past conflicts and their victims. And there is also the visit to the permanent exhibition rooms of the museum, from the Bronze Age to the Middle Ages and the Renaissance, from the century of Louis XIV, the "Sun King", through to Napoleon and Napoleon III, from the aftermath of the defeat at Sedan through to both world wars and the life of General de Gaulle. Together they relate a breathless story of a nation in arms across eras and political regimes.
It is my sincere hope that this guide will excite enthusiasm among visitors and expand their knowledge. I hope too that it will allow those who have not had time to see everything to leave with ... a certain regret and, above all, a desire to return.
I bid a warm welcome to one and all while emphasising that, depending on the year, the season and the time of day, the Invalides and the Army Museum can offer visitors a new face and fresh revelations.

General Christian Baptiste
Director of the Army Museum

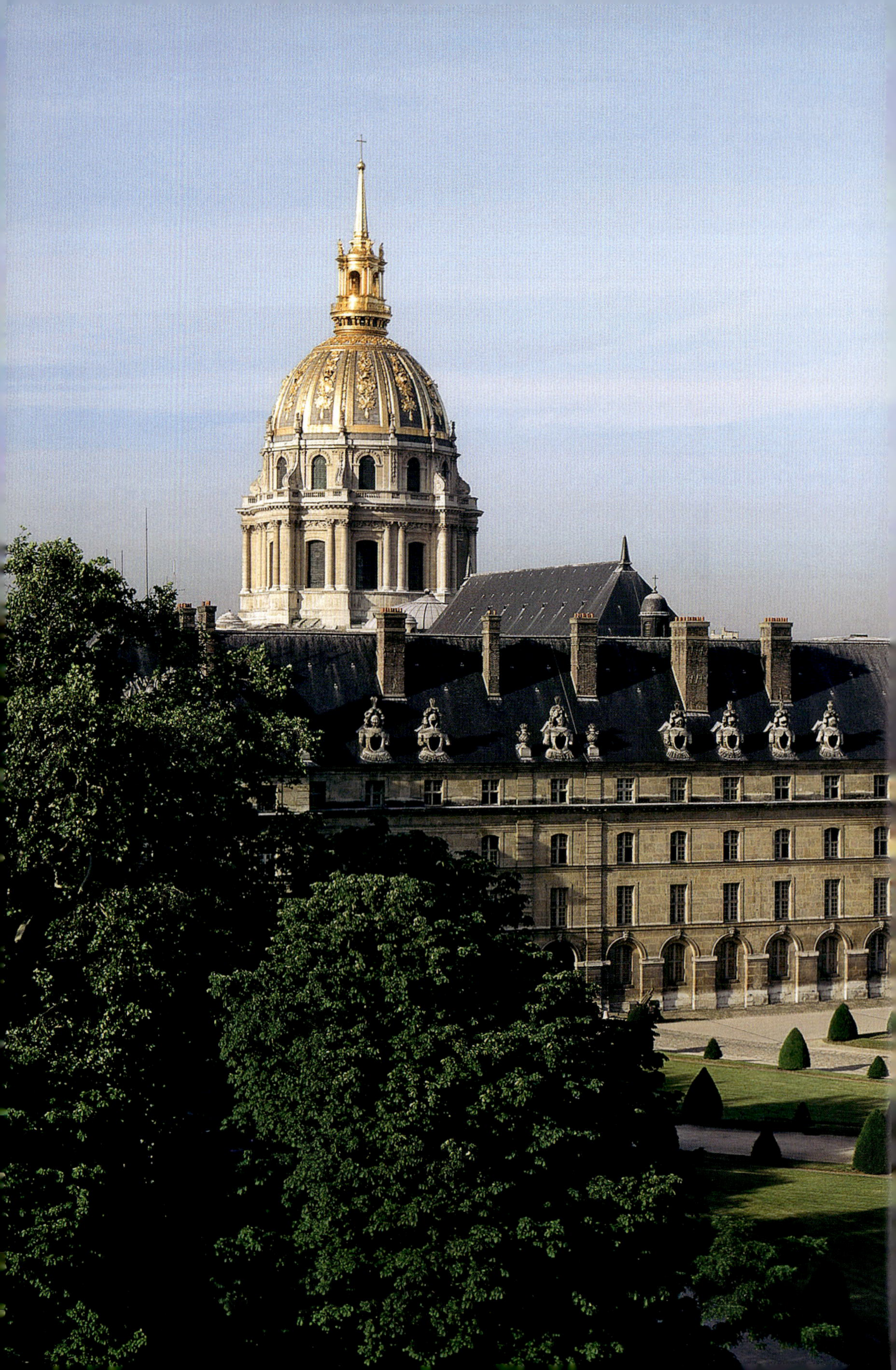

The Hôtel des Invalides

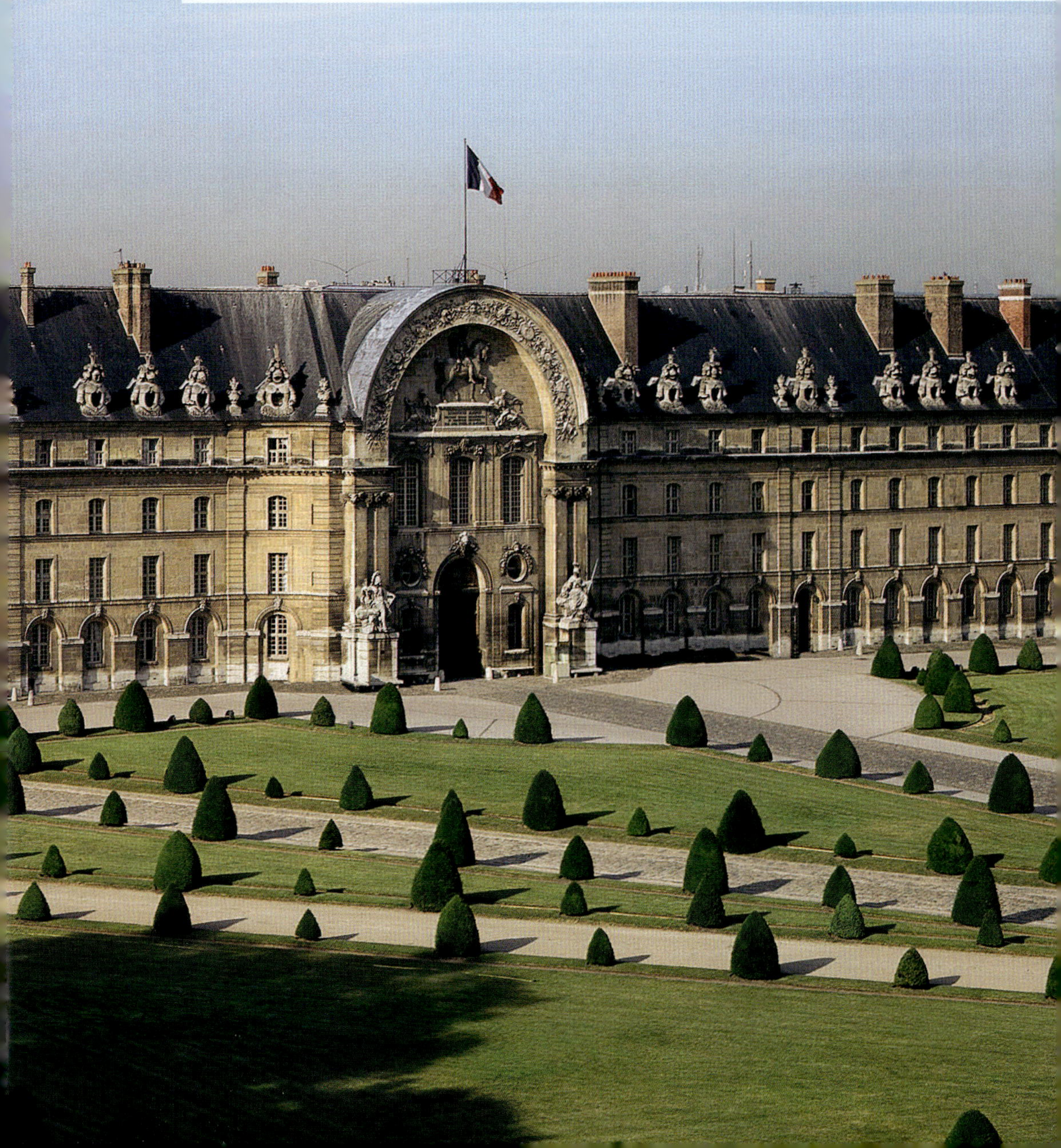

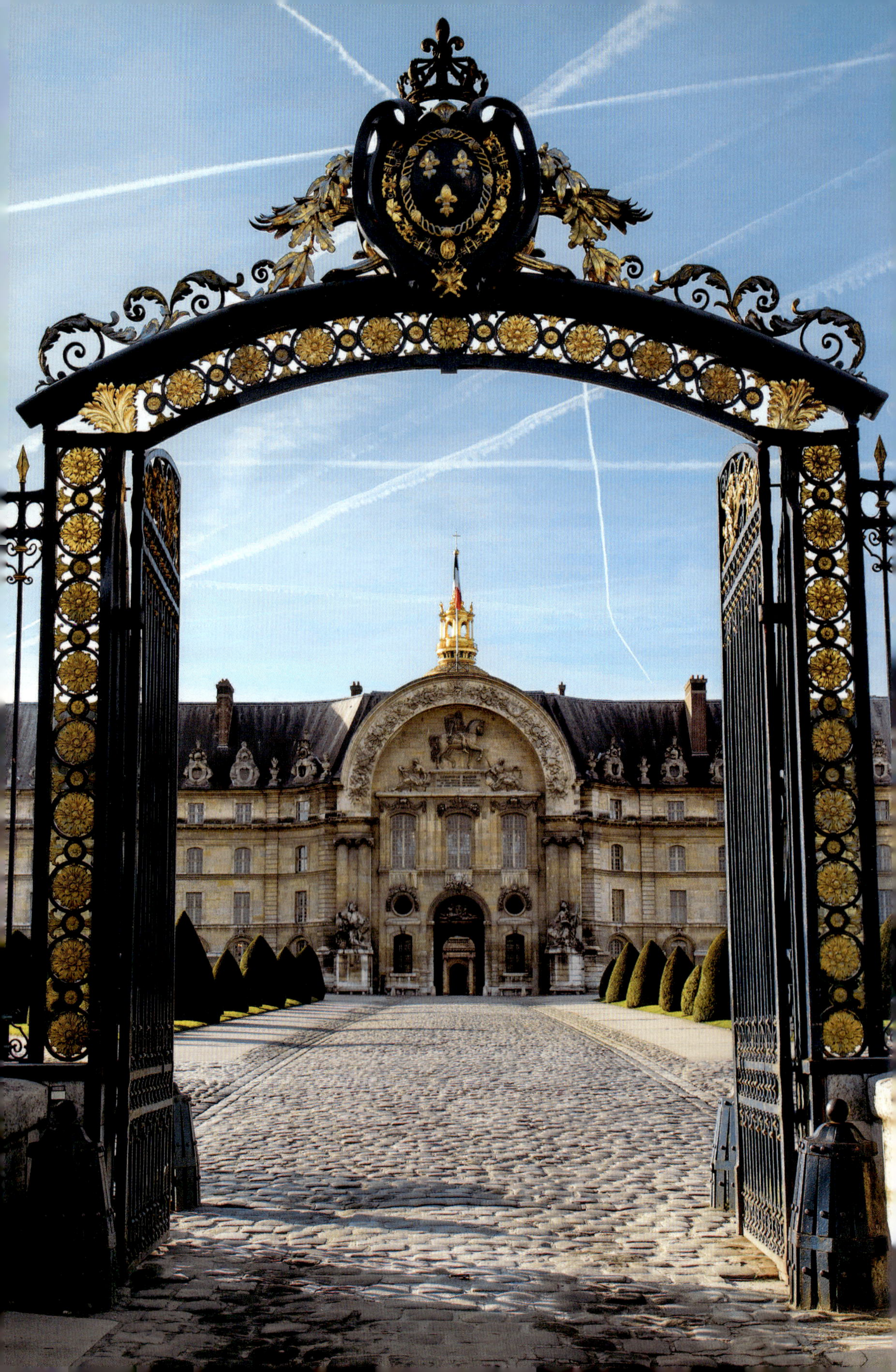

The Hôtel des soldats

Known the world over due to the presence of Napoleon I's tomb, the Hôtel des Invalides is nonetheless the work of Louis XIV. Built in the 17th century to accommodate wounded, sick or elderly soldiers, it would later witness the events of the Revolution before being transformed into a military pantheon of France in the 19th century.

Today, the Invalides is one of the French capital's major heritage, tourist and cultural sites, while continuing to fulfil its mission as a hospital. It is also a place of remembrance which hosts national ceremonies, of both a civil and military nature.

A major foundation by Louis XIV

"Among the various establishments that we have created in the course of our reign, there is none that is more useful to the state than that of the Hôtel Royal des Invalides," declared Louis XIV (1638 -1715) in his will. He would be King of France from 1643 until his death.

Before the Invalides existed, soldiers suffering from injury or disease or who were too old to remain in the ranks faced a miserable fate. With no means of support, many were reduced to wandering the streets cap in hand. Others were taken in by abbeys but had difficultly adapting to monastic life, punctuated as it was by prayer and silence. The monks, for their part, had considerable difficulty keeping these former soldiers in order. The institutions established by Henri IV and Louis XIII to accommodate veterans failed to stay the course.

Louis XIV was keen to improve the lot of disabled soldiers. Besides a willingness to perform an act of Christian charity towards an impoverished class of men, the King intended to make the military profession more appealing so as to facilitate recruitment and expand his army. In 1670, he decided on the construction of an establishment providing accommodation and care for soldiers unable to continue the profession of soldiery. This policy benefited from a favourable financial situation.

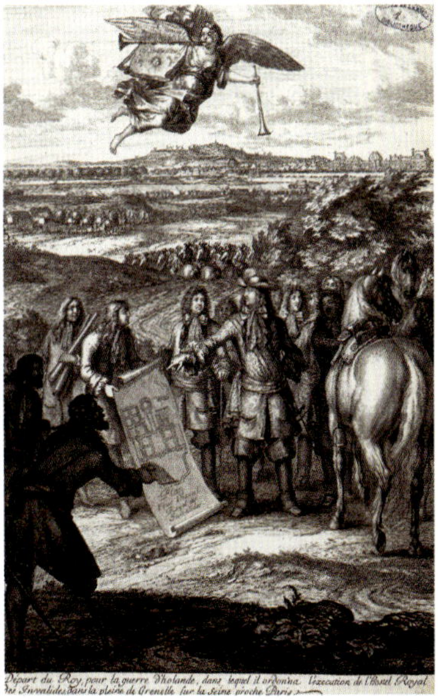

Robert Bonnard, *The King's departure for the Dutch war, in which he ordered the construction of the Hôtel Royal des Invalides*, etching on paper, 0.41x0.276 m, 1683. In fact, the decision to found the Hôtel dates from before the war with Holland, which began in 1672.

Left-hand page:
North gate of the Hôtel des Invalides.

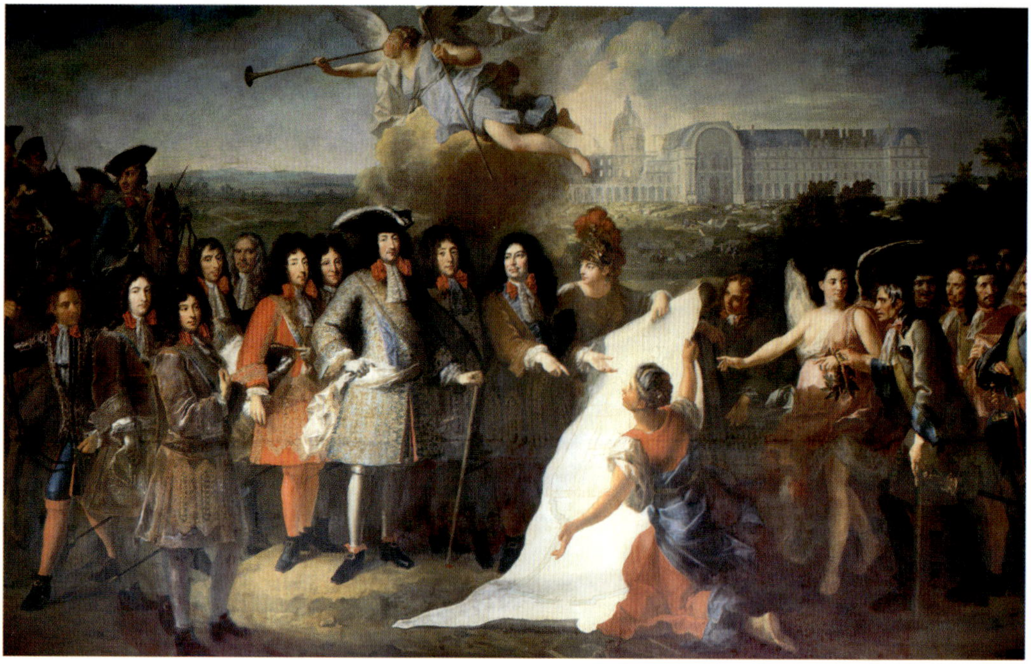

Pierre Dulin, *Establishment of the Hôtel Royal des Invalides*, Tapestry cartoon, circa 1710, 353x578 cm.
In the centre, Louvois presents the plan for the Invalides to Louis XIV who is holding a cane. In the left foreground are the architects Liberal Bruant and Jules Hardouin-Mansart. On the right, a group of disabled soldiers led by Glory.

Louis XIV and disabled soldiers

"... We felt that it was no less worthy of our devotion than our justice, to rescue from poverty and begging the poor officers and soldiers among our troops, who having grown old in the service, or been maimed in past wars, were not only unable to continue serving, but also to fend for themselves; and that it was reasonable that those who freely put their lives at risk and spilled their blood in defence and support of this monarchy [...] should enjoy the rest they have assured our other subjects, and thus spend the remainder of their days in tranquillity."
Extract from the April 1674 royal edict.

The location chosen for the future building was the Plaine de Grenelle, a vast stretch of land located close to Paris, along the Seine. The sodden ground was drained in preparation. The proximity of the river allowed for the rapid delivery of construction materials and the regular supply of the Hôtel.
The Minister of War, the Marquis de Louvois (1641-1691), was responsible for overseeing the project. Its implementation was initially entrusted to the architect Libéral Bruant (1635-1697), who designed a general grid, organised around a large central courtyard extended southwards by the church.
The plan of the Invalides was inspired by that of El Escorial, a monastery and royal palace built between 1563 and 1584 near Madrid, at the initiative of Philip II of Spain (1527-1598). Although both ensembles share a common austerity and strong religious dimension, there was no attempt at imitation on the part of the French architects. It should also be noted that, unlike El Escorial, the Hotel des Invalides has never served as the sovereign's residence.

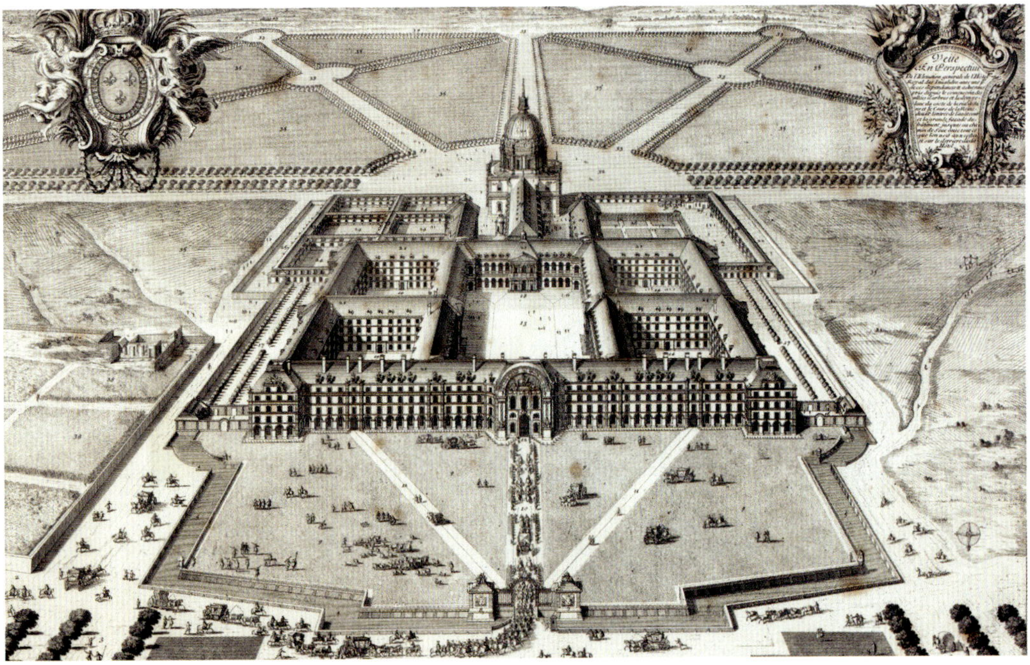

Pierre Lepautre, *Perspective view of the Hôtel Royal des Invalides*, etching and engraving, circa 1680, 0,402x0,557 m.
The plan of the Invalides juxtaposes several closed courtyards in the manner of monasteries and convents.

Thirty years of construction

Construction of the Invalides took over thirty years, from 1671 to 1706, and comprised two periods.
After the laying of the foundation stone in 1671, work rapidly progressed. As early as October 1674, the first residents moved into the establishment. All buildings except the church and the hospital were then completed.
In spring 1676, Louvois replaced Liberal Bruant with Jules Hardouin-Mansart (1646-1708), who oversaw building of the Eglise des Soldats largely by following the plan of his predecessor, between 1676 and 1679. The new architect focused his efforts on construction of the Eglise Royale, known as the Eglise du Dôme, which is exclusively his work. The walls and the dome were completed in December 1690. It would take a further sixteen years to finish the gilding and painted decorations, in a context of severe financial difficulties caused by war spending. On 28 August 1706, Louis XIV officially opened the Dôme des Invalides.

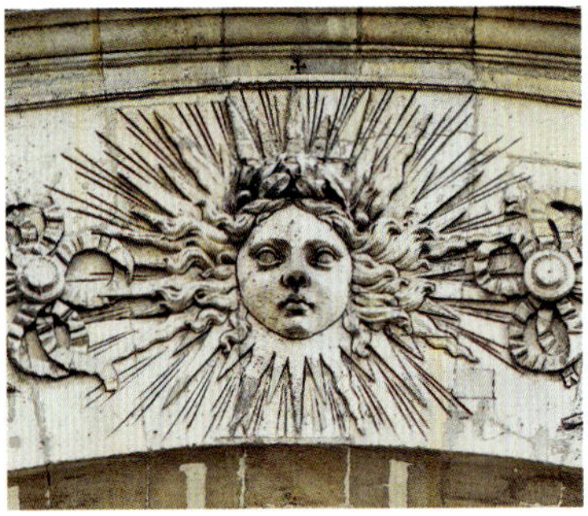

North façade of the Hôtel des Invalides: the sun with a human face, the emblem of Louis XIV.

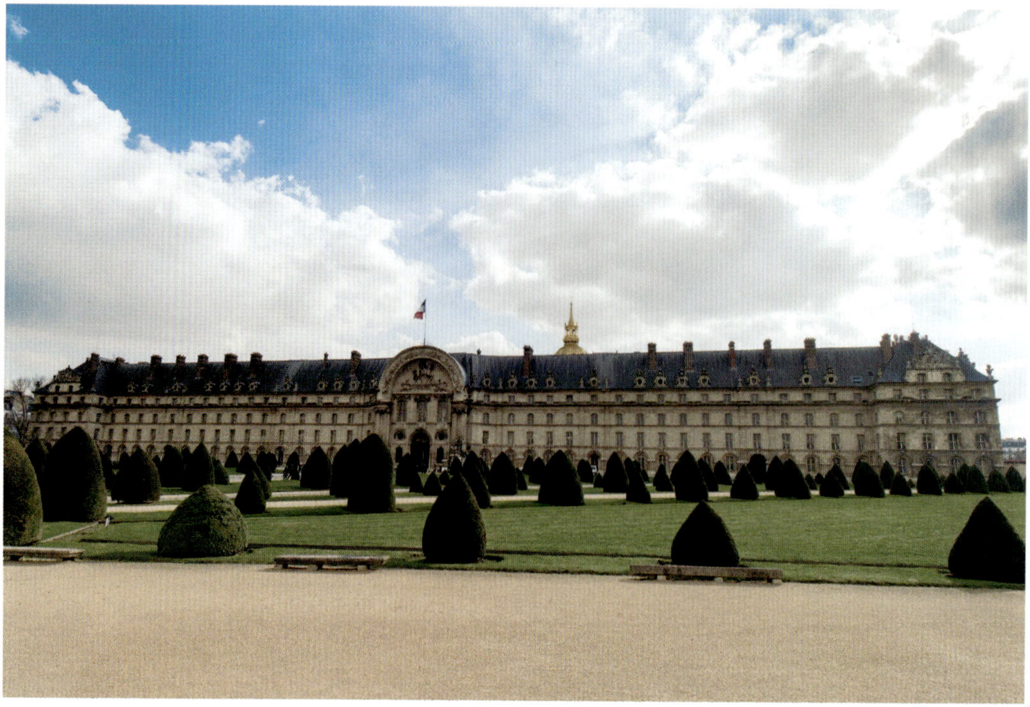

The north façade of the Invalides. Large and austere, it is divided into two symmetrical parts on either side of the central pavilion, on which stands a semi-circular arch.

The north façade

The north façade is one of the oldest parts of the Invalides. It offers a magnificent view to visitors arriving by the esplanade from which it is separated by a forecourt lined with defensive ditches. Cannons set out above them, near the front gate of the Hôtel, form the triumphant battery of the Invalides.

Almost 200 metres long and 22 metres high, the north façade is an imposing and austere ensemble which is symmetrical in form. Its decoration celebrates Louis XIV, the warrior king.

The most detailed part of this decoration is to be found on the central pavilion. In fact, the arch surmounting it is adorned with trophies, among which features a radiant sun, the emblem of Louis XIV. Under the arch, the King himself is represented on horseback, like a Roman emperor, flanked by Prudence on the left and Justice on the right. This sculptured group is the work of William Coustou (1677-1746). The Latin inscription on the pedestal translates as follows: "Louis the Great, by royal

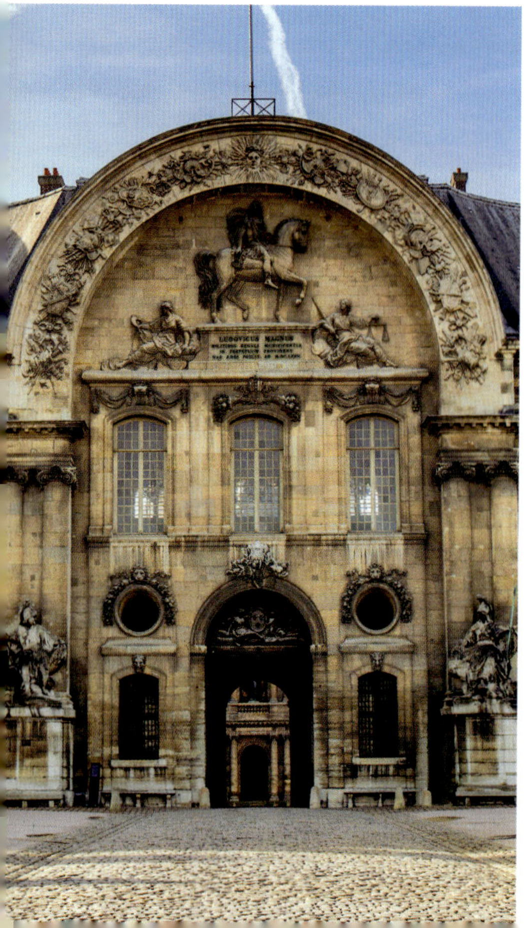

Central pavilion of the north facade.

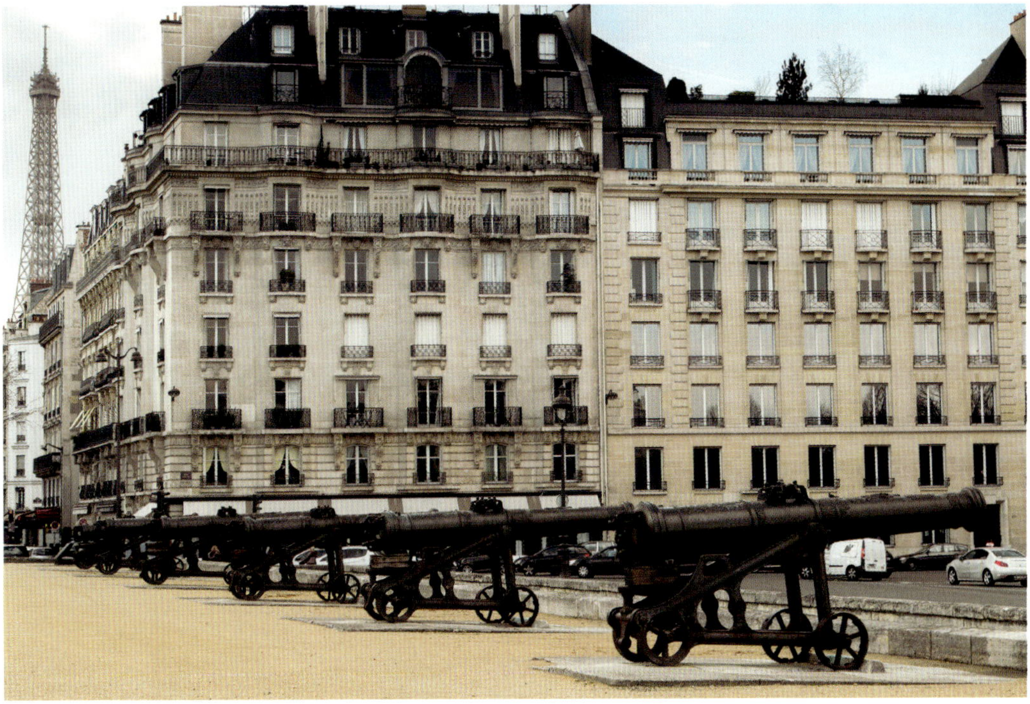

Cannons of the triumphal battery. Since the 17th century, salvoes have been fired from the Invalides to mark important events: military victories, the beginning of a new reign and now the investiture of presidents of the Republic.

munificence for his soldiers and providing for the continuation of time, founded this building in the year 1675." Fleur-de-lys, the emblem of the French monarchy, can be seen on the tympanum of the door. Its stone arch bears the head of Hercules wearing the skin of the Nemean lion. The Greco-Roman hero, embodying strength, is a traditional symbol of royal authority. The entrance to the central pavilion is flanked by statues of two Greco-Roman gods of war, Athena-Minerva on the right and Ares-Mars on the left.

Other notable elements of the north façade's decoration include the trophies of dormer windows, recalling the victorious campaigns of the Sun King. Finally, mascarons or sculptured masks present on the arches of the ground-floor windows, relieve the austere aspect of this part of the monument.

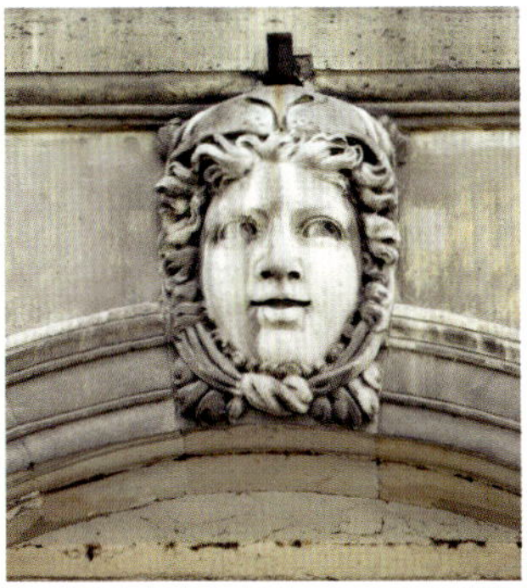

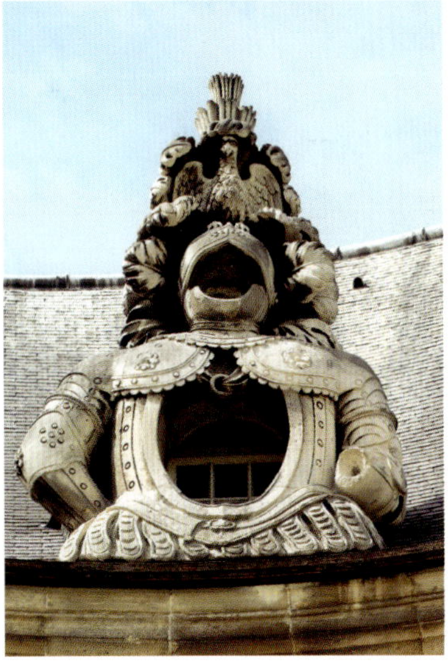

Dormer window on the north façade. Its decorative feature consists in a trophy composed around armour.

A mascaron on the north façade.

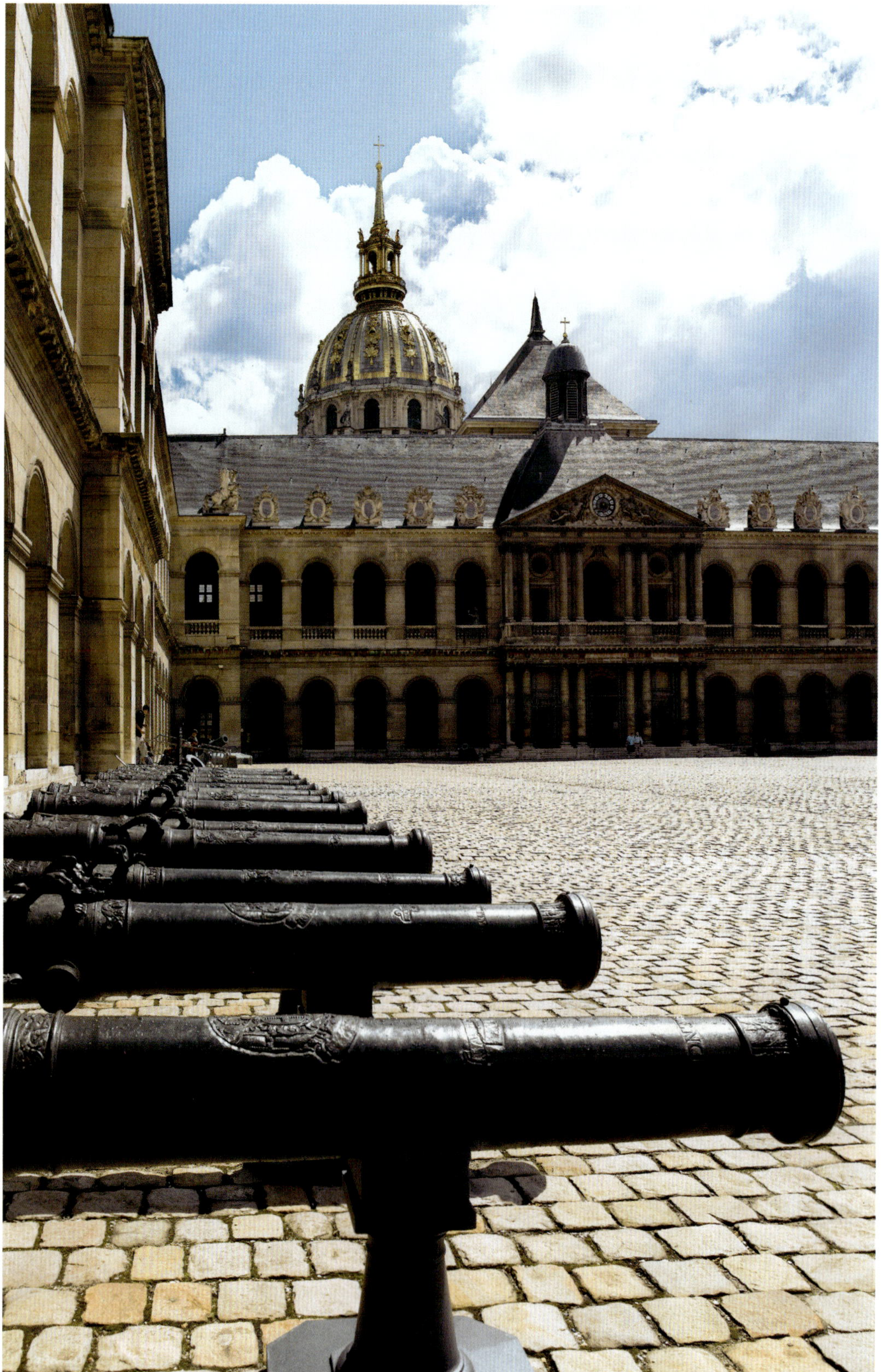

The main courtyard

The door of the central pavilion of the north façade offers access to the main courtyard. 102 metres long and 64 metres wide, this is the largest courtyard of the Invalides. It is fully paved and enclosed by four main buildings, each with two levels of arcaded galleries.
The extremely austere decoration of this courtyard is reserved for the upper parts of the façades, featuring sixty dormer windows with war-like motifs, combining symbolic figures with trophies consisting of weapons, armour, flags and musical instruments. The significance of these ornaments with multiple variants has not been fully elucidated. On the cornices of the corner pavilions, statues of horses trampling prisoners are positioned between each series of dormer windows.
The sundials on the west, north and east porticos of the court date from the 18th century. They respectively indicate the time in the morning, at mid-day and in the afternoon.
Under the upper central arch of the south façade, stands the statue of Napoleon I, the work of Charles Émile Marie Seurre (1798-1858). Positioned at the top of the column of the Grande Armée, Place Vendôme in 1833, it was removed in 1863 before being transferred to the Invalides in 1911.
Along the façades, bronze cannons are presented in batteries. They belong to the collections of the Army Museum. and trace the history of the French land artillery from the 17th to the 19th centuries.
The upper gallery of the courtyard is accessible to the public via two staircases at the southeast and southwest corners. The walls of this gallery are covered with plaques commemorating conflicts which the French army has participated in since the 19th century.

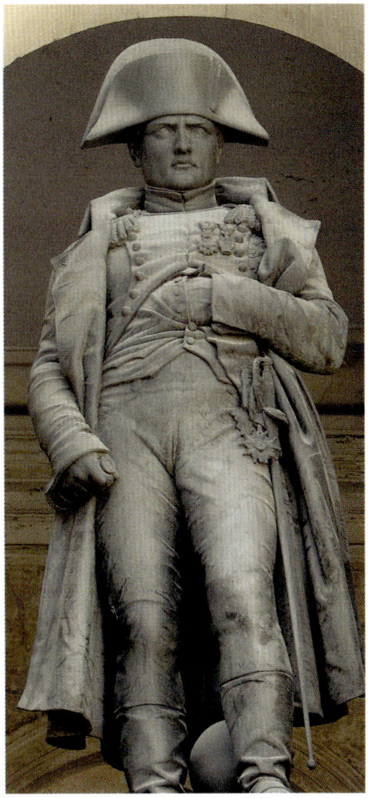

Charles Émile Seurre *Statue of Napoleon I* 1833, bronze, h. 4 m, 4,500 kg.
The Emperor is represented in accordance with the legend, in his uniform of Colonel of Les Chasseurs de la Garde, with hat, frock coat and the characteristic position of the hand.

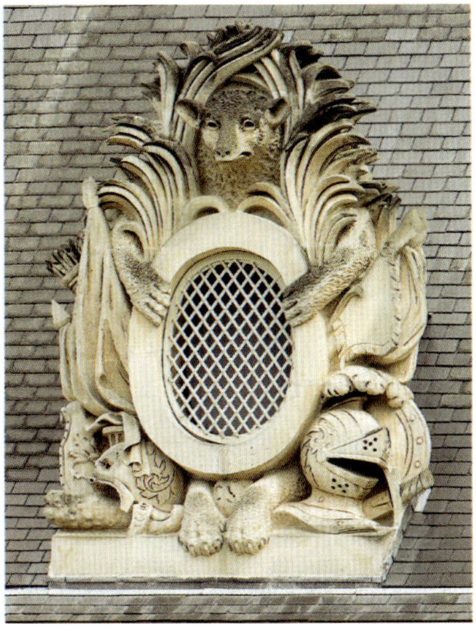

The so-called Louvois dormer window.
The opening of this dormer window on the main courtyard is held by the legs of an animal, probably a wolf whose head emerges from tall grass. This decor is traditionally interpreted as a discreet allusion to the role of Louvois in the construction of the Invalides ("loup" meaning "wolf" in French).

Left-hand page:
The courtyard of the Invalides.

The daily lives of residents

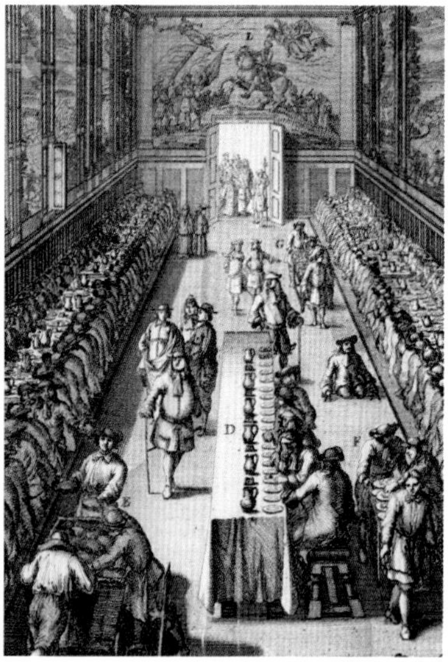

Lepautre Jean (1618-1682), *View of one of the canteens of the Hôtel des Invalides*, etching and engraving, circa 1680-1681, 0.42 x 0.565 m, detail. Punished soldiers, deprived of wine, eat at the so-called "water drinkers" table in the centre.

In the 17th and 18th centuries, the Hôtel fulfilled several functions which made it a fully-fledged military, religious and medical establishment.

The Invalides was first and foremost a military barracks (housing more than 4,000 men in 1714). The soldiers slept in rooms of four to six beds and ate their meals in four canteens each seating four hundred. They had to respect discipline, wear the uniform and take exercise when physically possible.

The Invalides was also a convent where daily participation in the religious services was mandatory, as well as prayers. These religious services were provided by twelve and subsequently twenty priests.

The Invalides was also an "hôtel", that is to say, a hospital. Sick and wounded soldiers received care and each had their own bed, a degree of comfort which was very rare for the period. Due to the presence of older officers and soldiers, the Hôtel also served as a retirement home for veterans.

The Revolution

The events of the French Revolution had a massive impact on everyday life in the Invalides.

On the morning of 14 July 1789, the people of Paris entered the building and seized thousands of muskets and several cannons, weapons which were immediately used to storm the Bastille.

A few years later, because of its monarchical character, the institu-

Jean-Louis Prieur (1759-1795), *Taking of arms at Invalides, the morning of 14 July 1789*, Drawing, 18th century, 0.18 x 0.241 m.

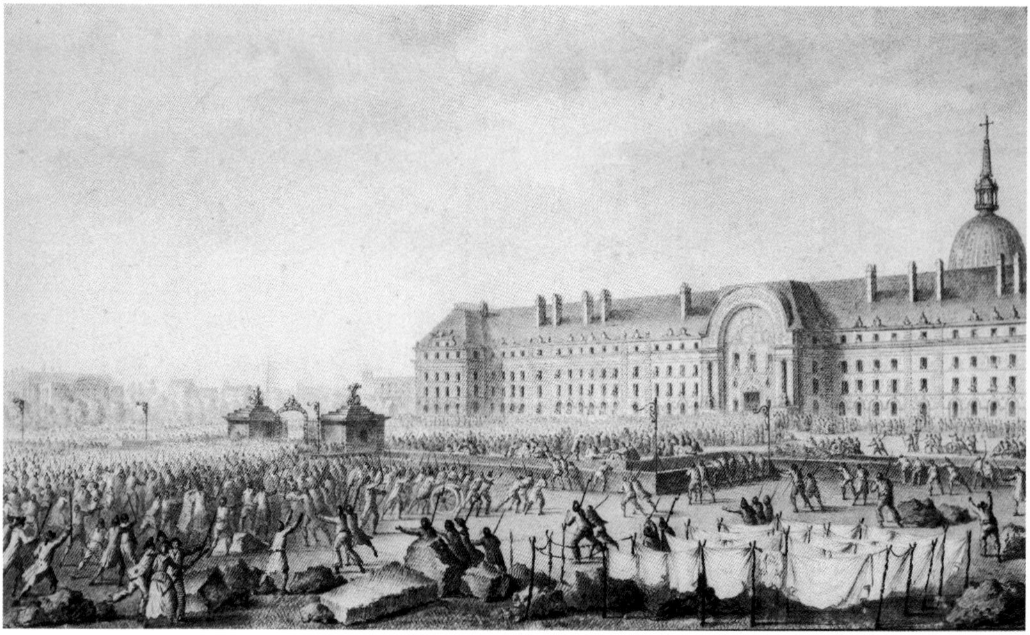

tion came in for heavy criticism and was threatened with demolition. Royal and religious symbols were concealed or destroyed. Catholic worship ceased to be celebrated in the Eglise St. Louis, which was henceforth used to store flags captured from the enemy. Order returned to the Hôtel under the Directory (1795-1799) and the Consulate (1799-1804). In 1801, Bonaparte reintroduced religious ceremonies.

The military pantheon of France

Napoleon transformed the former Hôtel Royal into a pantheon of French military glory by organising the transfer of Turenne's tomb to beneath the dome in 1800. Then, in 1807, he ordered the transfer of Vauban's heart (see p. 27). This function as a necropolis was extended in 1840 by the decision to build, under the Dome once more, the tomb of Napoleon I himself (see p. 28 and following).
The Panthéon des armées extends to the Eglise des Soldats, particularly in the vault beneath its nave. Reserved for the governors of the Invalides before the Revolution, it was opened to high-ranking military leaders in the 19th century.
The tradition continued in the 20th century: the Caveau des gouverneurs became the resting place of Claude Joseph Rouget de Lisle, author of *La Marseillaise*, as well as prominent leaders of the armies of the Great War (Maunoury, Fayolle, Mangin, etc.) and the Second World War, such as Marshalls Leclerc and June. The tombs of Marshalls Foch and Lyautey were also placed under the dome (see p. 33).

Arms for the Revolution

"We arrived at the Invalides at about two of the afternoon and discovered a great crowd [...]. I followed the throng to reach the vault where the weapons were kept. On the stairs of the cellar, having come across a man with two muskets, I took one from him and began climbing back upwards; but at the top of the stairs, the crowd was so great that all those ascending were forced back down to the vault."
The day of Jean-Baptiste Humbert, watchmaker, who was the first to ascend the towers of the Bastille, Paris, 1789.

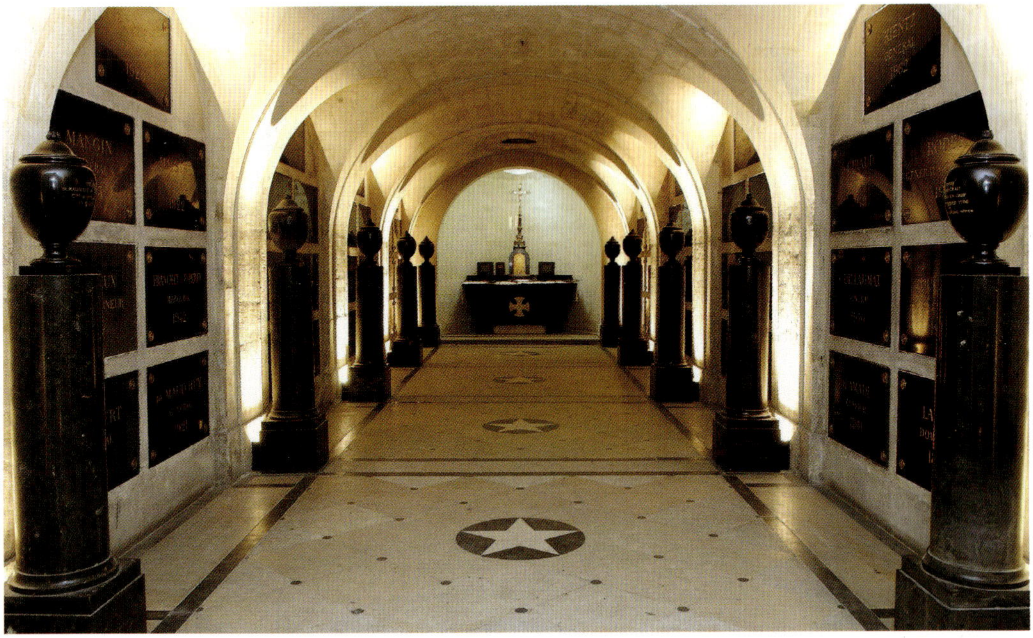

Caveau des gouverneurs des Invalides (restricted access). Located under the Eglise des Soldats, it comprises ninety-three tombs.
The star decorations on the ground indicate the presence of generals and Marshalls.

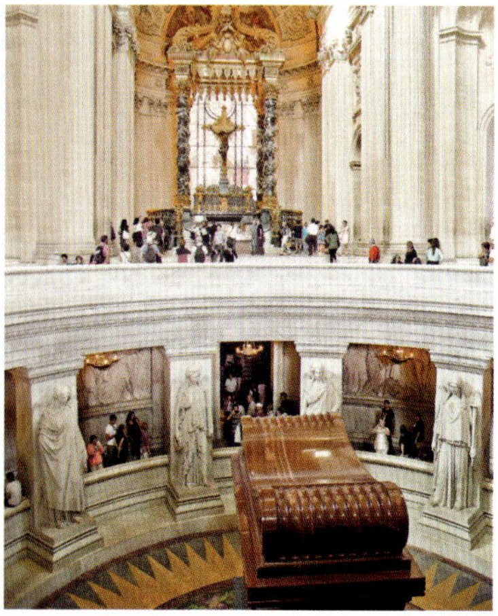

Dôme des Invalides: public visiting the tomb of Napoleon I. This area is managed by the Army Museum.

A prestigious museum

The museum is the newest feature of the Invalides. It was introduced between 1776 and 1777, when the royal collection of relief maps or models of fortified towns left the Louvre for the Hôtel's attic, where it remains to this day.

The decisive change came in 1871, when the Musée d'Artillerie, housed in the cloister of Saint-Thomas-d'Aquin in Paris, moved into the canteens of the west wing of the Invalides. In 1896, the building was also used to host the Musée historique de l'Armée, modelled on the military pavilion of the Universal Exhibition of 1889. The merger of the two institutions gave rise to the Army Museum in 1905.

Two other museums joined the site in 1960 and 1970: the Musée de l'Ordre de la Libération and the Bibliothèque de documentation internationale contemporaine (BDIC).

The Invalides today

All the original functions of the Invalides have survived through to the present day.

The army still stamps its authority on the building through the presence of the military governor of Paris. Several military and civilian agencies are also established there.

The main courtyard of the Invalides, 30 September 2011: ceremony celebrating the two hundred years of the Sapeurs-Pompiers de Paris (Paris Fire Brigade).

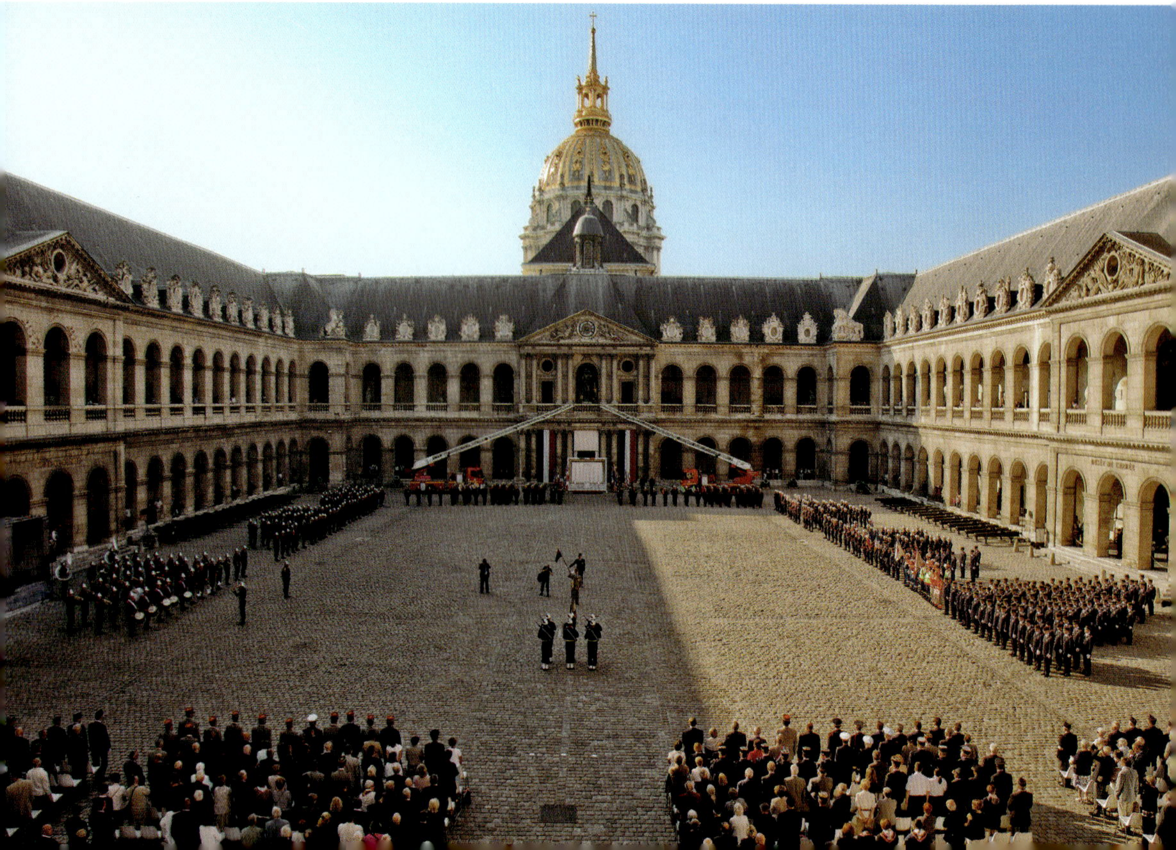

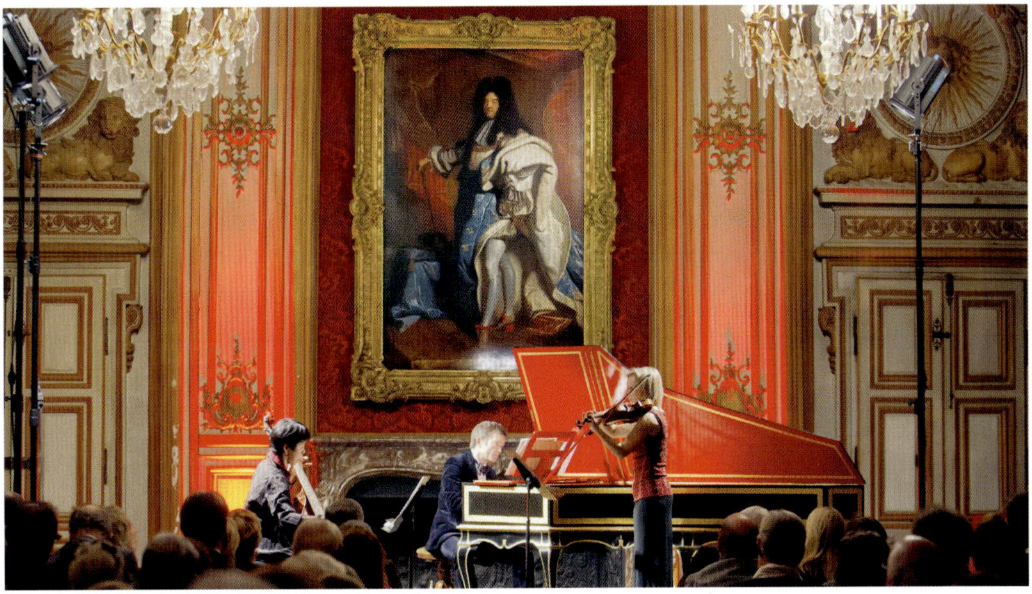

Concert by Les Talens Lyriques in the Grand Salon of the Army Museum on 21 November 2012. Receptions, cocktail parties and musical performances are held regularly in this prestigious space. The portrait of Louis XIV is a reproduction of a work painted by Hyacinthe Rigaud in 1701.

The Invalides continues to fulfil an important religious role through masses, weddings, christenings and funerals, celebrated in the Eglise des Soldats, which in 1986 became the cathedral of the diocese to the French armies.

The hospital mission continues within the Institution nationale des Invalides, with an advanced medical and surgical centre and a retirement home for war invalids.

The museum dimension is now at the heart of the monument's activities. The Invalides is one of the most visited sites in Paris due to the presence of the tomb of Napoleon, a universally famous historical figure, but also the attractiveness of the museums. Among these, the Army Museum is to the fore with its five hundred thousand objects and attendance of close to one and a half million visitors each year, mostly foreigners. In rooms which were fully renovated between 2000 and 2010, it presents the history of the French Army from the 13th century through until 1945, resituated in its European and global context.

Throughout the year, ceremonies are held in the main courtyard during parades, tributes, awarding of military decorations. The President of the Republic regularly attends. The Hôtel also serves as a setting for many shows, concerts, screenings, conferences and symposia, which means that this monument dating from over 300 years ago remains a favoured venue for outstanding events.

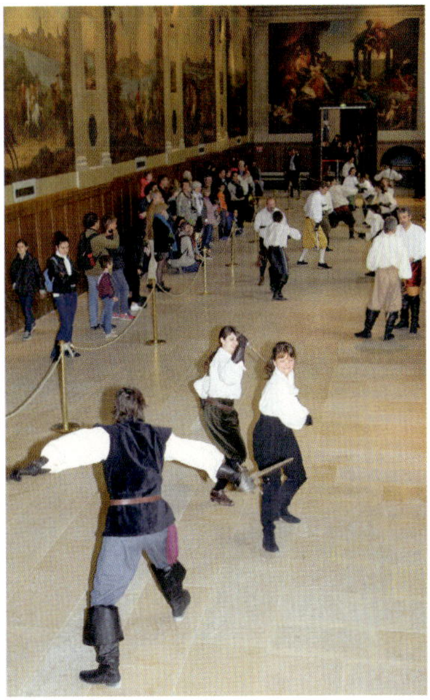

Fencing demonstration by the Cyclone troupe in the Army Museum's Turenne room, April 2014.

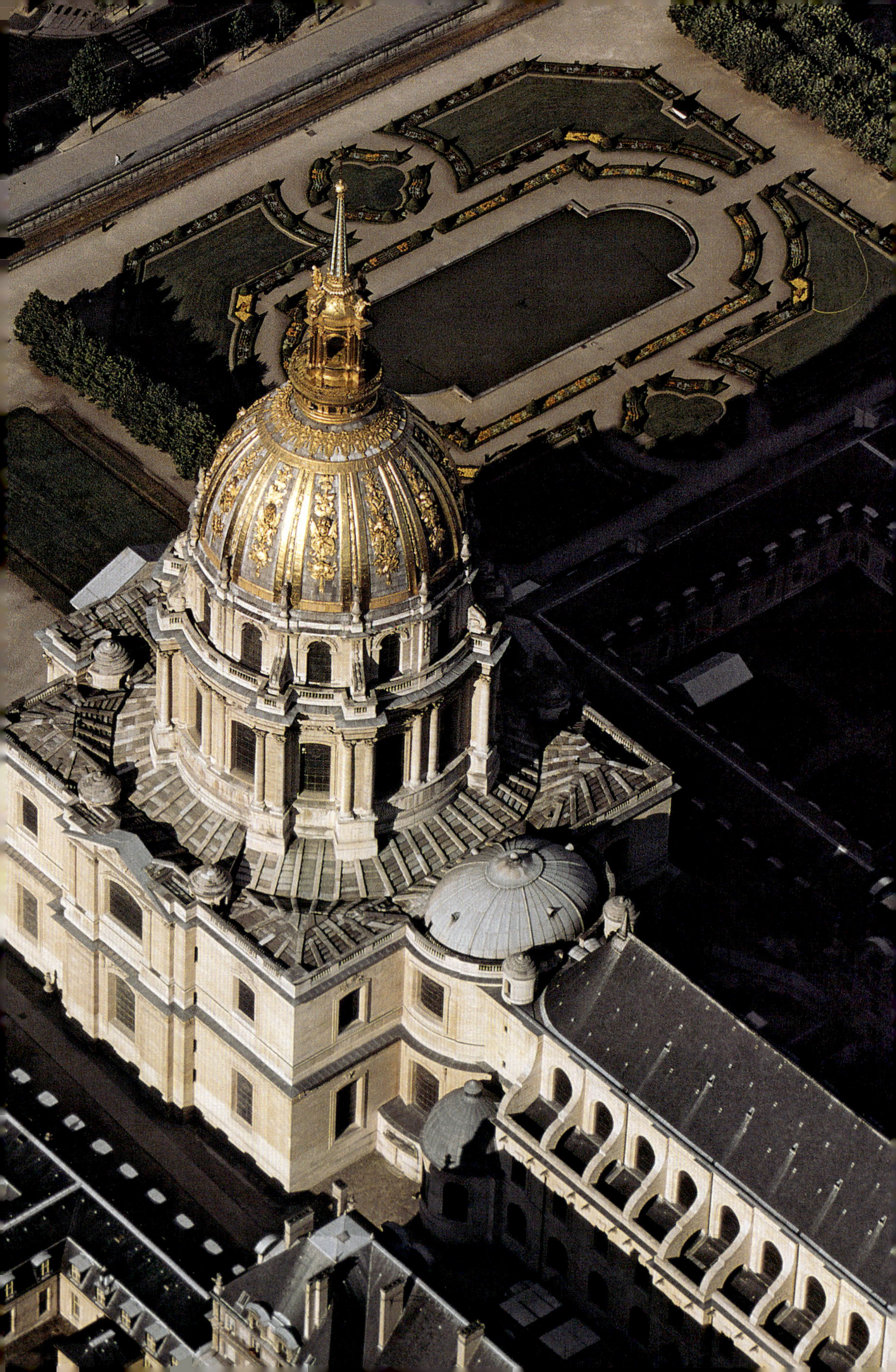

From church to necropolis

Are there one or two churches at the Invalides? The original plans suggest the notion of a single church, dedicated to St. Louis and structured around the Dome. However, as of its construction, the two parts of the building evolved very differently: although the daily religious celebrations took place in the northern part, the Dome, to the south, was reserved for royal visits and official ceremonies. In the 19th century, this trend was confirmed by the construction of Napoleon's tomb under the Dome and the installation of an atrium between the two altars. The use it was assigned gave rise to the names of "Eglise des Soldats" and "Eglise du Dôme".

The Eglise des Soldats

This structure has the shape of a long nave covered with a barrel vault. Nine bays with arcades provide access to side galleries overlooked by elevated galleries.

Left-hand page:
Aerial view of the Invalides' twin churches, namely the Eglise du Dôme (top left) and the Eglise des Soldats (bottom right).

Vault, galleries and flags of the Eglise des soldats now the Cathédrale Saint-Louis des Invalides.

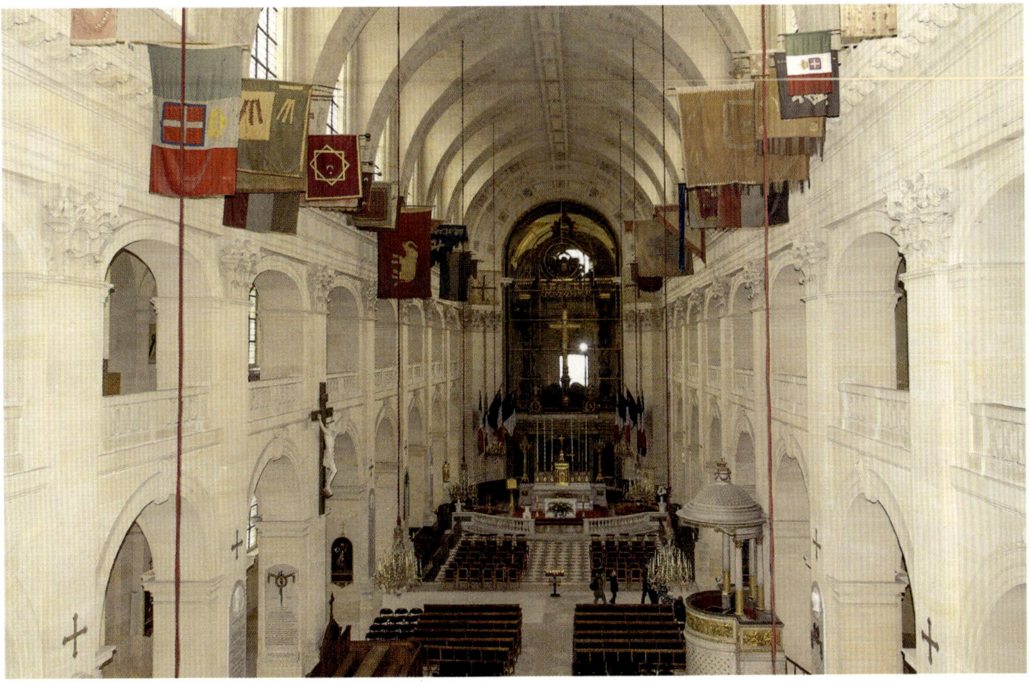

Flags captured from the enemy have been presented since the French Revolution. Today, more than seventy emblems belonging to the collections of the Army Museum are displayed at the bottom of the arch.

Most of the plates fixed to pilasters bear the names of governors of the Invalides and military leaders buried in the vault beneath the altar and the nave (see p. 17).

The Eglise des Soldats also houses several monuments related to the two world wars: the chapel of the generals dead in service and the urn containing soil from the battlefields of 1914-1918; another urn, from the Voie de la Liberté (1944), contains earth from American cemeteries in France.

Now the seat of the diocese to the armies, the Eglise des Soldats became the Cathédrale St. Louis in 1986. Religious services and concerts are held there all year round as well as funerals for well-known figures or soldiers who died during military service.

A masterpiece of Parisian architecture, the Invalides dominates the southern part of the Hôtel.

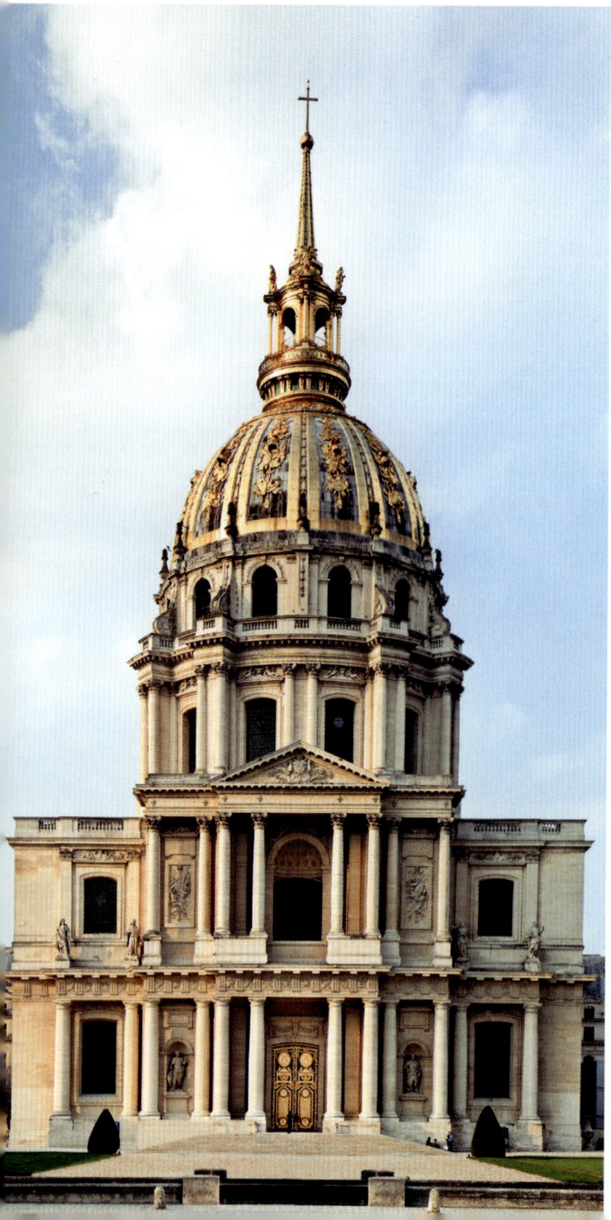

The Eglise du Dôme

The Eglise du Dôme is the former Eglise royale des Invalides. The work of the architect Jules Hardouin-Mansart, it was built then decorated between 1677 and 1706. In the Historical description of the Hôtel royal des Invalides (1756), Father Perau described it as "one of the world's finest examples of architecture".

With its dazzling aesthetics and harmonious proportions, this monument rises to a height of 110 metres. It consists of three elements which are superimposed, from bottom to top: a quadrangular structure, a drum and a dome.

The façade of the Dome, facing south, consists of two levels, above which stands a terrace.

The drum also comprises two floors whose many windows serve to light up the building's interior. The first of these floors is reinforced by a line of protruding double columns.

The dome, which rests on the drum, is topped by a lantern surmounted by a spire.

The outdoor decoration of the Dome

Majestic and elegant, the Dôme des Invalides differs greatly from the austere north façade. Yet there is a considerable unity of theme between it, the courtyard and the façade of the Dome, in that all three architectural ensembles exalt the military glory of Louis XIV and the monarchy.

On the first level of the Dome's façade appears the Doric order, the oldest and least ornate of the Greek orders. This sobriety is broken by the front door, gilded with fine gold and carved, bearing the royal emblems: fleurs-de-lys, suns with human faces, double interlinked Ls for Louis XIV and the initials (SL) of the church's patron, St. Louis. A statue of the monarch can be seen to the left of the door. Created by Nicolas Coustou (1658-1733), it symbolises the alliance of the French monarchy and Catholicism. On the right, a statue of the Emperor Charlemagne (800-814), created by Antoine Coysevox (1640-1720), highlights the imperial ancestry of the kings of France.

On the second level of the façade, we can note the Corinthian order, characterised by its column capitals decorated with acanthus leaves. The statues of the four cardinal virtues (Strength, Justice, Temperance and Prudence) are positioned there.

The Dome is covered with 550,000 sheets of gold leaf and the total weight is a mere 12.6 kg. The last regilding operation took place in 1989, the bicentenary of the French Revolution. Trophies adorn the Dome, while fleurs-de-lys cover the spire topped with a cross.

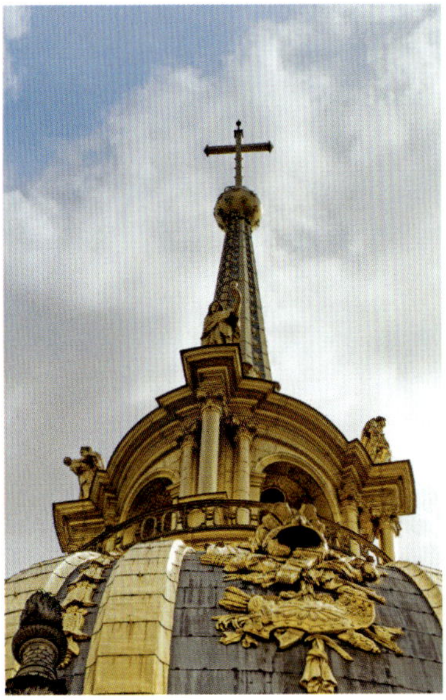

The trophies, lantern and golden spire of the Dome. Each gold leaf is 0.2 microns thick. The cross reminds us that the monument is a former church.

From left to right, statue of St. Louis after Nicolas Coustou, golden door of the Dome and Statue of Charlemagne after Antoine Coysevox.

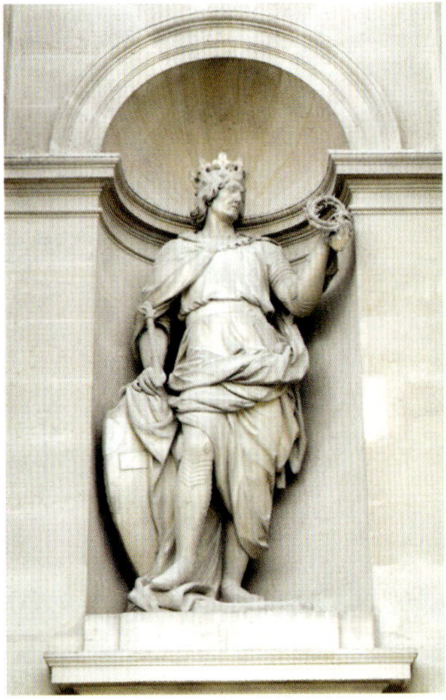

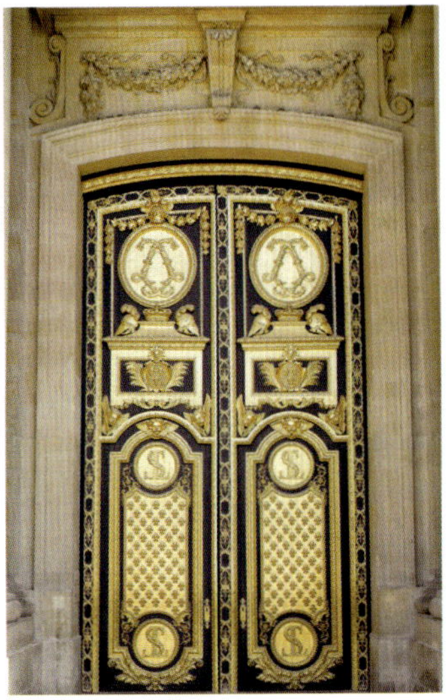

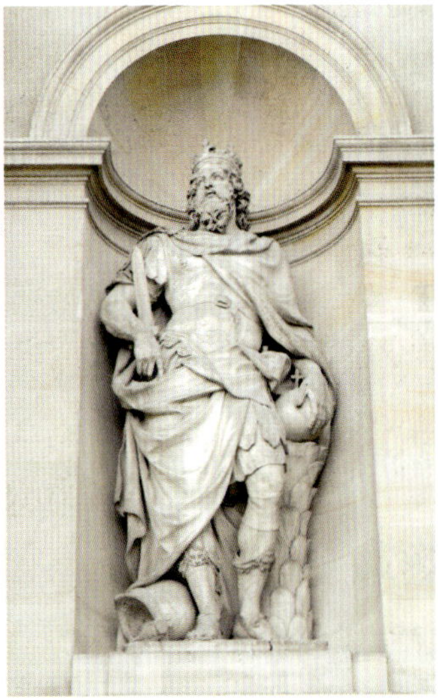

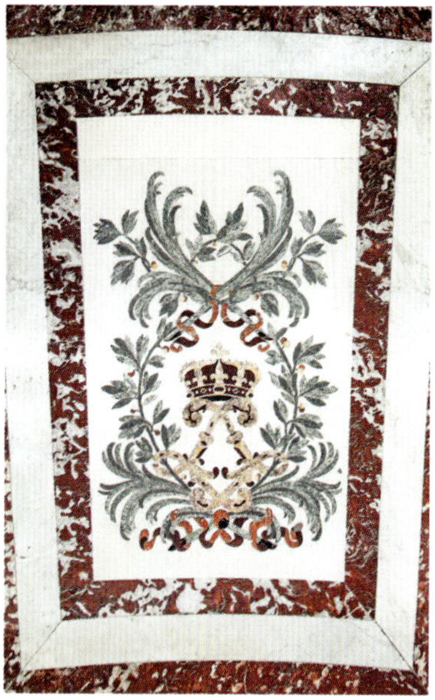

The marble floor of the Eglise du Dôme. In one of the compartments of the circular frieze, the royal crown with fleurs-de-lys is positioned on the double capital *Ls* of Louis XIV.

Inside the Dome

The internal structure of the dome, within a square of 55 metres on each side, follows a plan in the shape of a Greek cross. The large central excavation, where the tomb of Napoleon lies, preceded the construction of the building (see p. 29).

The altar dates from the 19th century. Covered by a canopy with twisted columns, it replaced the former altar which was destroyed during the Revolution.

The four corner chapels are dedicated to the Fathers of the Church, St. Augustine, St. Ambrose, St. Gregory and St. Jerome. The bas-reliefs of the vaults bear religious, royal and military symbols. Others evoke the life of St. Louis. The Corinthian style is present on the pillars and pilasters. The two middle chapels are dedicated to the Virgin Mary and St. Therese. The suns and double Ls of Louis XIV are displayed on their vaults.

Murals depicting the four Evangelists, by Charles de La Fosse (1636-1716), extend the Dome drum. At its base, against a fleurs-de-lys background, twelve portraits of the kings of France, from Clovis to Louis XIV, remind us of the long-standing tradition and continuity of the monarchy (see next page).

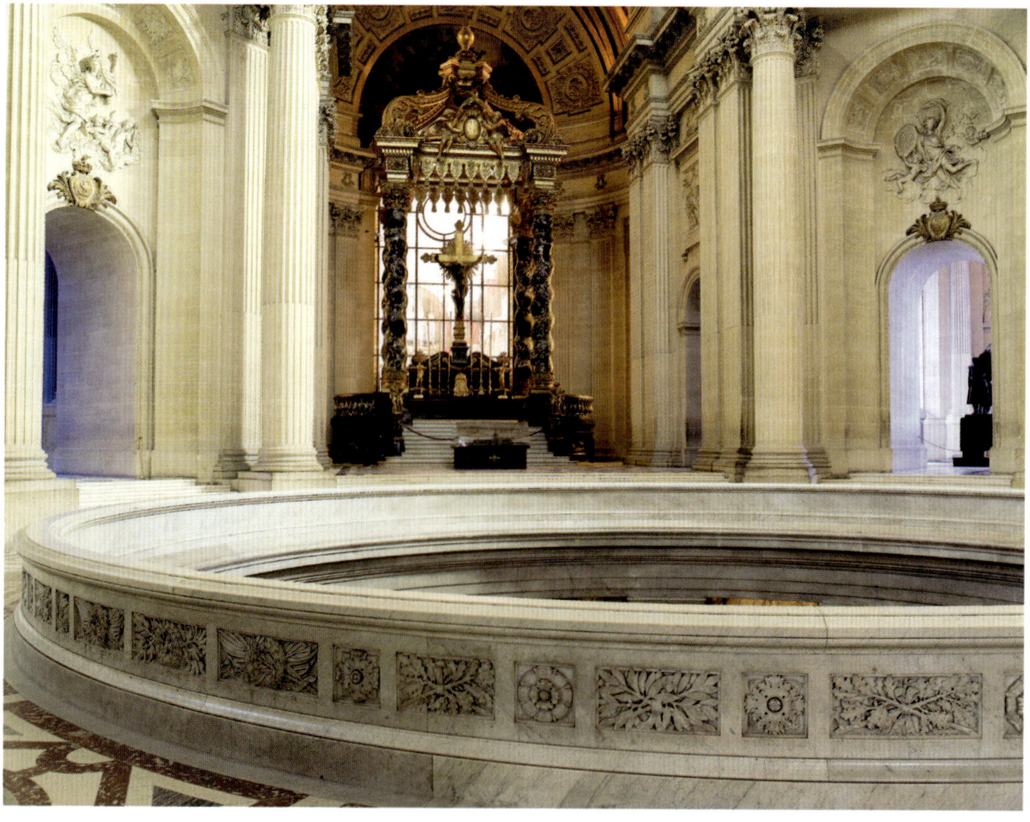

The Eglise du Dôme: the altar with canopy, the corner chapels and the opening housing the tomb of Napoleon.

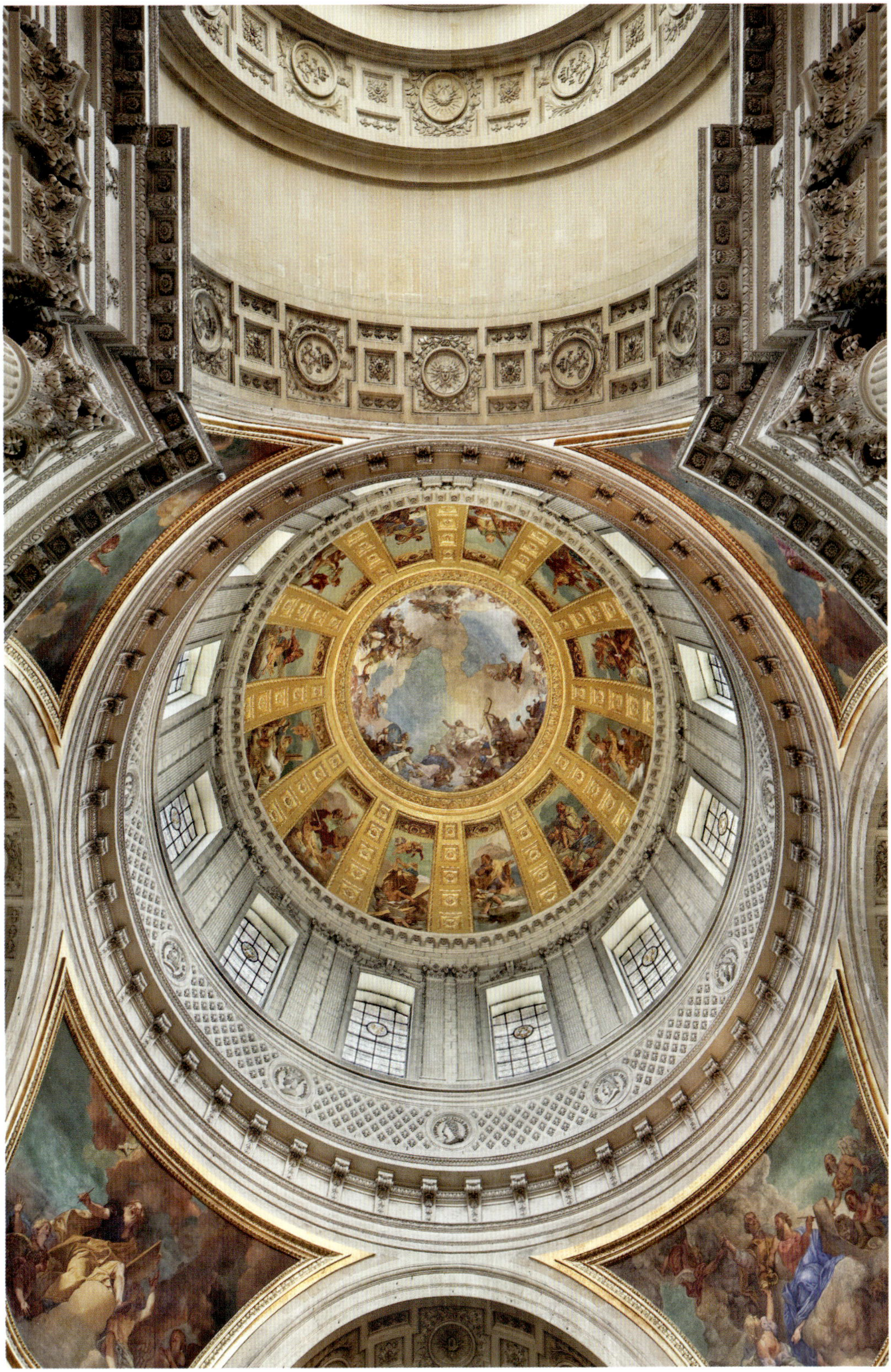

The Eglise du Dôme: interior view of the drum and the dome.

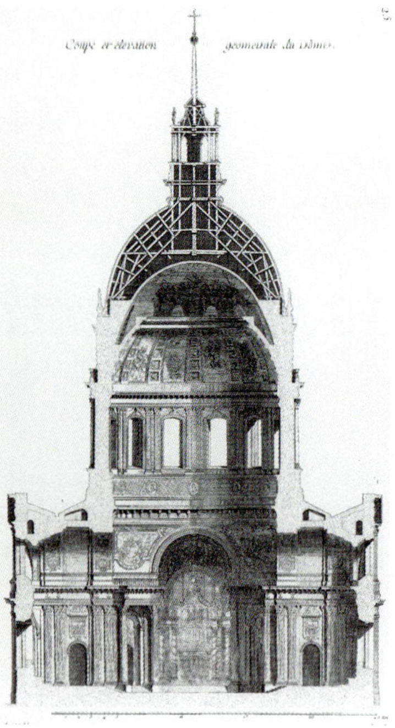

Cross section and geometric elevation of the Dome. Diagram of Abbot Perau, *Historical description of Hôtel royal des Invalides*, Paris, Desprez, 1756, 0.5 x 0.29 m. The two superimposed cupolas of the Dôme des Invalides are clearly visible.

Rising to 80 metres above the ground, the highest part of the dome consists of two cupolas (see the diagram opposite): the open lower one conceals the second floor of the drum's windows from inside the building. This inventive method makes it possible to direct the light coming from these windows towards the calotte of the second closed cupola, which covers the first.

The alliance between the monarchy and the Catholic Church, a theme which already features in the decorative programme of the ground floor and the drum, is developed on the double cupola.

The lower cupola is decorated with portraits of the Twelve Apostles, painted by Jean-Baptiste Jouvenet (1644-1717). Each of these portraits is 14 metres high.

The main decoration of the Dôme des Invalides is located on the calotte of the upper cupola, on which a large pictorial composition shows St. Louis offering his sword to Christ. The work of Charles de La Fosse, this scene powerfully embodies the notion of the divine nature of royal power, which gives the sovereign the status of God's representative in his kingdom.

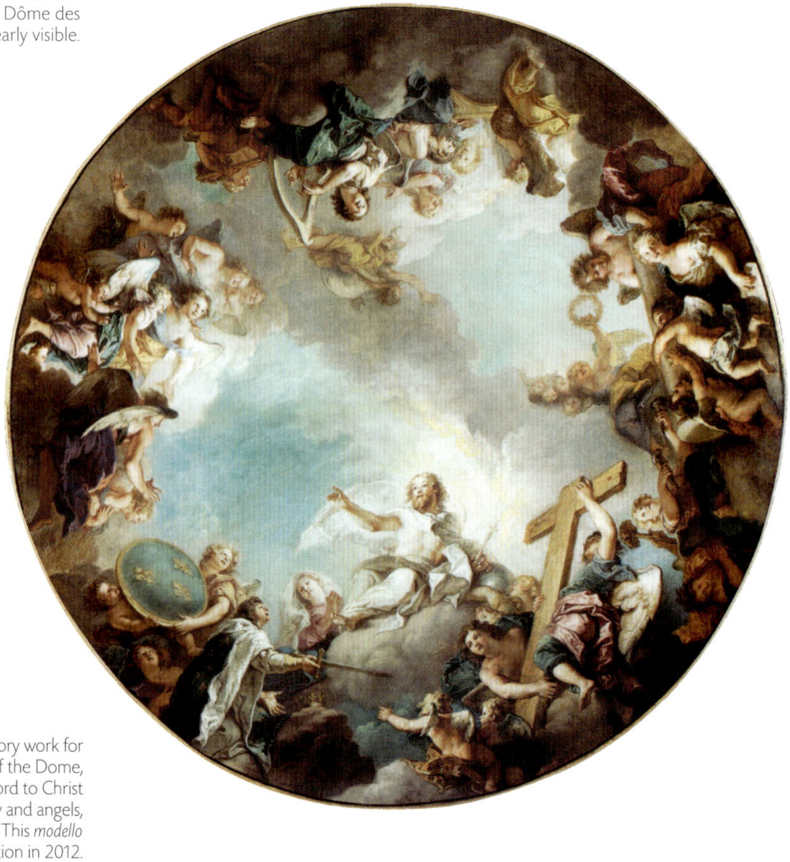

Charles de La Fosse, *modello* or preparatory work for the decoration of the cupola of the Dome, representing St. Louis offering his sword to Christ surrounded by the Virgin Mary and angels, circa 1702, oil on canvas, size 199.5 cm. This *modello* underwent extensive restoration in 2012.

Birth of the military pantheon: the tomb of Turenne and the funeral monument of Vauban

The tomb of Turenne and the funeral monument of Vauban are located in the middle two chapels of the Dome. The presence of these great men of war at the Invalides is due to Napoleon Bonaparte who, in 1800 and then in 1807, transformed the former Hôtel Royal into a pantheon of French military glory.

Marshall Turenne (1611-1675) was one of the most important army chiefs of the 17th century. His numerous victories after the French intervention in the Thirty Years' War, from 1635 to 1648, and during the continuation of hostilities against Spain until 1659, earned him the prestigious title of Marshall of France in 1643 and Marshall General of the camps and armies of the king in 1660. Honest and loyal, Turenne was very popular with his soldiers. Mortally wounded by a cannon ball in 1675, he was buried in the Basilica of Saint-Denis with the kings of France. His tomb was transferred to the Invalides on 22 September 1800, by order of the First Consul Bonaparte who, by so doing, assigned the Hôtel a new role: because it is the resting place of deserving soldiers, it is intended to receive the remains of the greatest military leaders. The tomb of Turenne, carved in the 17th century by Jean-Baptiste Tuby (1635-1700) and Gaspard Marsy (1624-1681), fits harmoniously into the Dome.

In 1807, a similar decision was taken by Napoleon, now emperor, concerning Prestre Sébastien de Vauban (1633-1707), the famous military engineer and architect, also Marshall of France. For the sake of symmetry with the tomb of Turenne, a funeral monument was built in front of it. This structure only contains Vauban's heart. The imperial regime wished to honour he who, through his fortresses, had defended his country. It also celebrated the author of *Projet d'une dixme royale*, a reform providing for a universal tax system, rejected by Louis XIV.

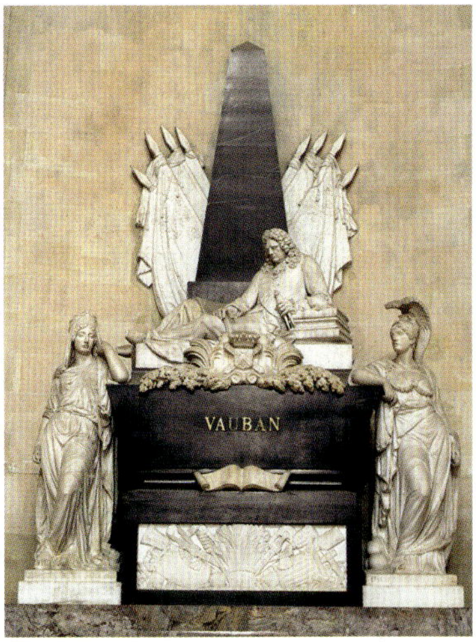

The Vauban monument built in 1807 was replaced in 1847 by that of Antoine Etex (1808-1888), created on the model of the tomb of Turenne, for the sake of harmony.

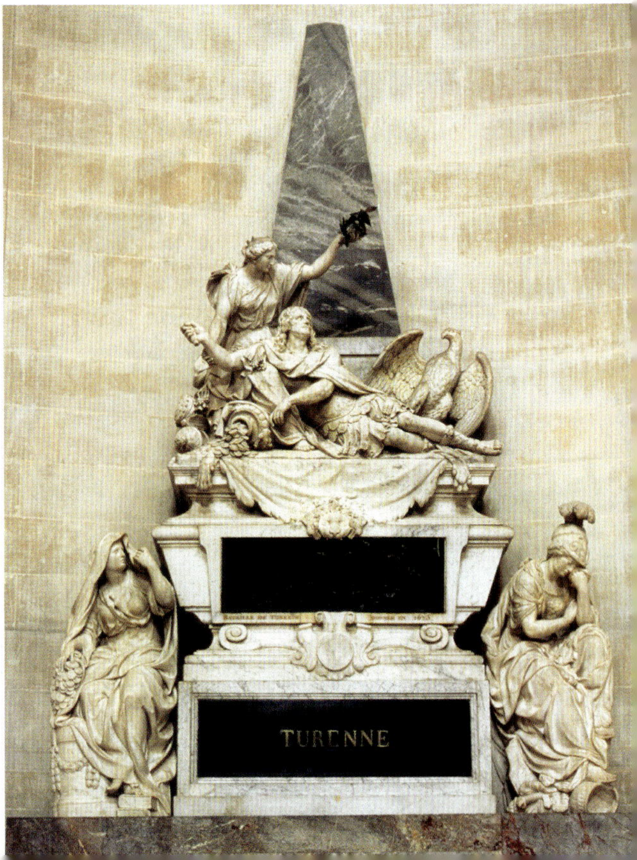

The tomb of Turenne.
Jean-Baptiste Tuby and Gaspard Marsy, 1675-1680.
The Marshall is supported by Christian hope. Wisdom, to the left, left and Value, to the right, are at his side.

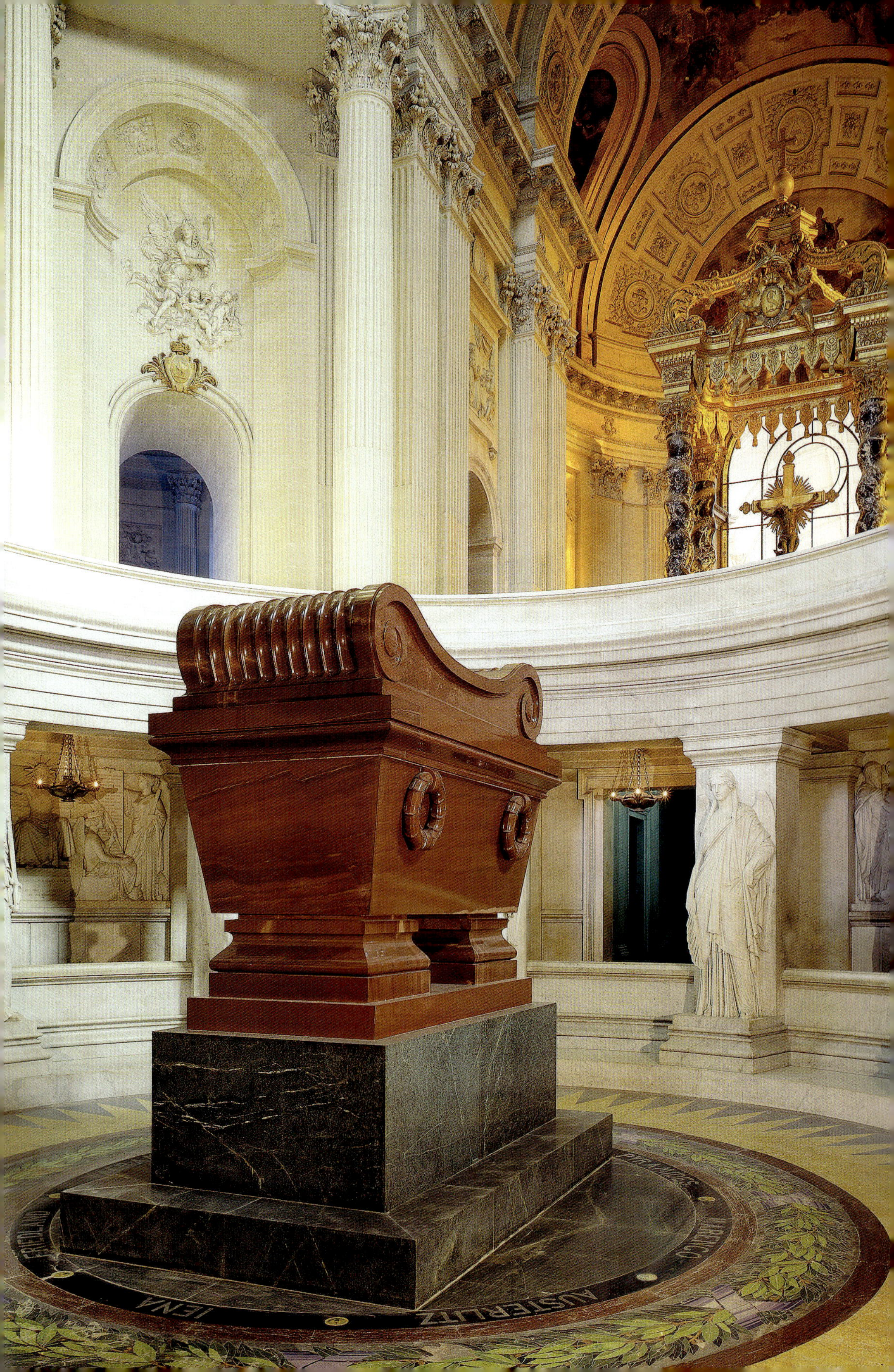
FRIEDLAND
IENA
AUSTERLITZ
MARENGO
PYRAMIDES

The tomb of Napoleon I

The decision to build the tomb of Napoleon I at the Invalides, taken in 1840, turned the Hôtel into an emblematic place of remembrance of the Emperor. This is particularly true for the former Eglise royale du Dôme, transformed into an imperial tomb. The transfer of Napoleon's ashes to the Invalides also confirms the building's role as a necropolis, where were buried many members of Napoleon's family, joined in the 20th century by Marshalls Foch and Lyautey.

From St. Helena to the Invalides: the return of the ashes

Napoleon Bonaparte (1769-1821), Emperor of the French under the name of Napoleon I (1804-1815), died on 5 May 1821, during his exile to the British island of St. Helena. He remained buried there until 1840, when the French king Louis-Philippe I organised, with the consent of Great Britain, the return to France of the Emperor's mortal remains. In a bid to increase his popularity, Louis-Philippe sent his third son, the Prince de Joinville to St. Helena on a mission to return with the remains of Napoleon. Because he is a great man of the army, his tomb would be built at the Invalides: "He must continue to reign and command in the establishment where the soldiers of the nation shall lie," explained Rémusat, Minister of the Interior.
The imperial coffin was placed in the Hôtel on 15 December 1840. The construction of the tomb began in 1842. It was eventually overseen by the architect of Italian origin, Louis Visconti (1791-1853), chosen because the project was the one which was most in harmony with the Eglise du Dôme. Work progressed slowly and Napoleon was only placed in the sarcophagus in 1861.

Left-hand page:
Tomb of Napoleon I, built from 1842 to 1853 by Louis Visconti, quartzite, green marble from Vosges, h. 5; w. 4; d. 2 m.

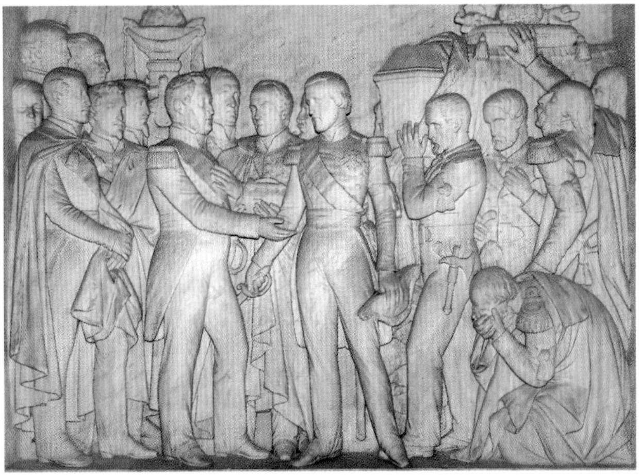

François Jouffroy (1806-1882), *King Louis-Philippe receiving the ashes of the Emperor under the Dôme des Invalides, 15 December 1840*, Bas-relief, marble, 1851.

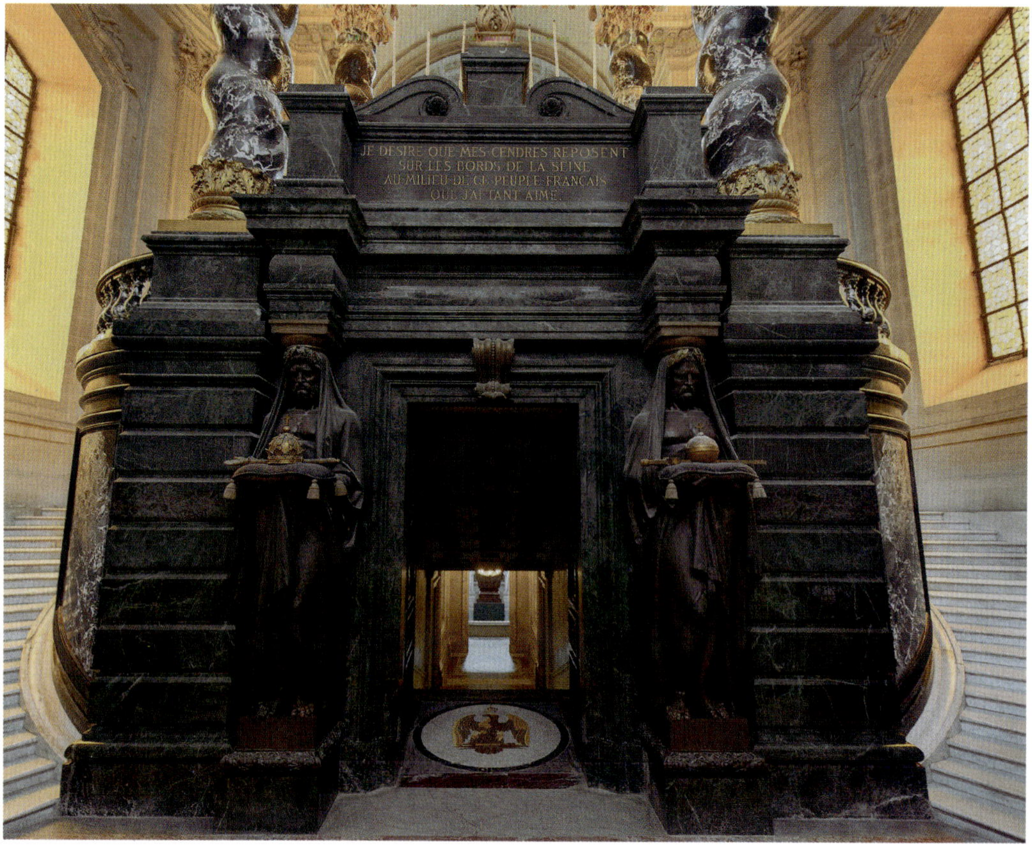

The entrance to the crypt

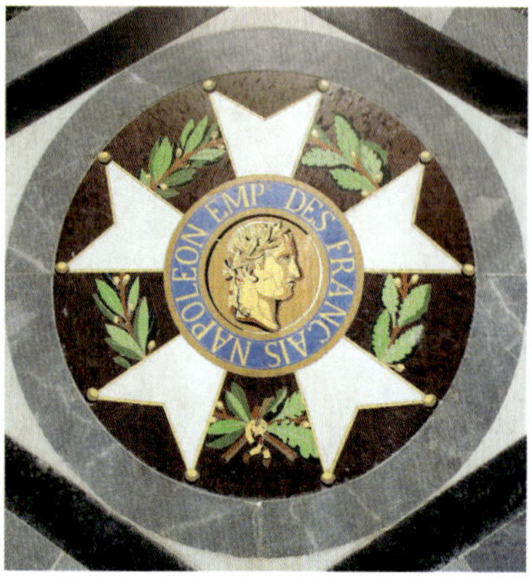

The lower floor landing of the staircase of the crypt: medallion decorated with the Legion of Honour with, in the centre, Napoleon in profile. The Légion d'honneur, created by Napoleon Bonaparte in 1802, rewarded deserving soldiers and civilians.

Stairs behind the altar of the dome provide access to the crypt or excavation of the tomb of Napoleon.

A monumental gate forms the entrance. It is flanked by two giant bronzes created by Joseph Duret (1804-1865). They are symbols of imperial power: on the right, the sword and orb (sphere surmounted by a cross, the emblem of the world), on the left, the crown and the hand of Justice.

An extract of Napoleon's will is shown on the upper part of the entrance: "I wish to be buried on the banks of the Seine in the midst of the French people whom I have loved so dearly." Although short on detail, this sentence allowed the July Monarchy to justify the choice of the Invalides - located near the Seine - as the burial place of the Emperor. During his lifetime, Napoleon thought he would be buried in Saint-Denis, the royal necropolis, but also in Lyon, the former capital of the Gauls, or Ajaccio, his hometown in Corsica.

The bronze door opens onto a staircase that leads to the crypt.

The sarcophagus

The excavation of the Dome by Visconti led to the creation of an open crypt, allowing the tomb to be illuminated by daylight. The rotunda thus created is 6 metres deep and 15 metres in diameter (21 metres with the outer gallery).
Napoleon's tomb occupies the central part. Its significant dimensions - 5 metres high, 4 metres long and 2 metres wide – match the scale of the building and the historical importance of the deceased. The base in green granite supports the sarcophagus in Finnish quartzite. This stone is very similar to porphyry whose dark red colour is reminiscent of the coats once worn by Roman emperors. The remains of Napoleon are in the sarcophagus and enclosed in five coffins fitted together, made of different materials: tin, mahogany, two in lead and ebony.
Neoclassical decoration of the tomb is sober. It pays tribute to the military glory of Napoleon Bonaparte. On the ground are the names of the eight greatest victories: Rivoli (1797), Les Pyramides (1798), Marengo (1800), Austerlitz (1805), Jena (1806), Friedland (1807), Wagram (1809) and Moscowa (1812). Laurel wreaths, distinctions for victors, are present on the ground, on the sarcophagus and in the hands of several of the twelve statues of victories against the pillars.

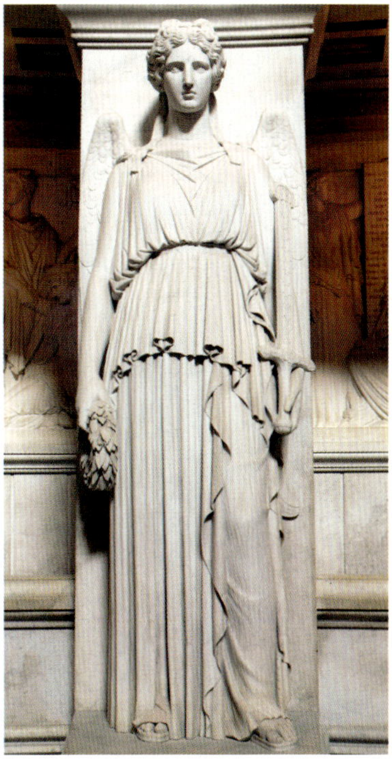

Jean-Jacques (called James) Pradier (1790-1852), Allegory of Victory, campaign in Italy (1800), white marble, h. 4 m, 1843-1852.

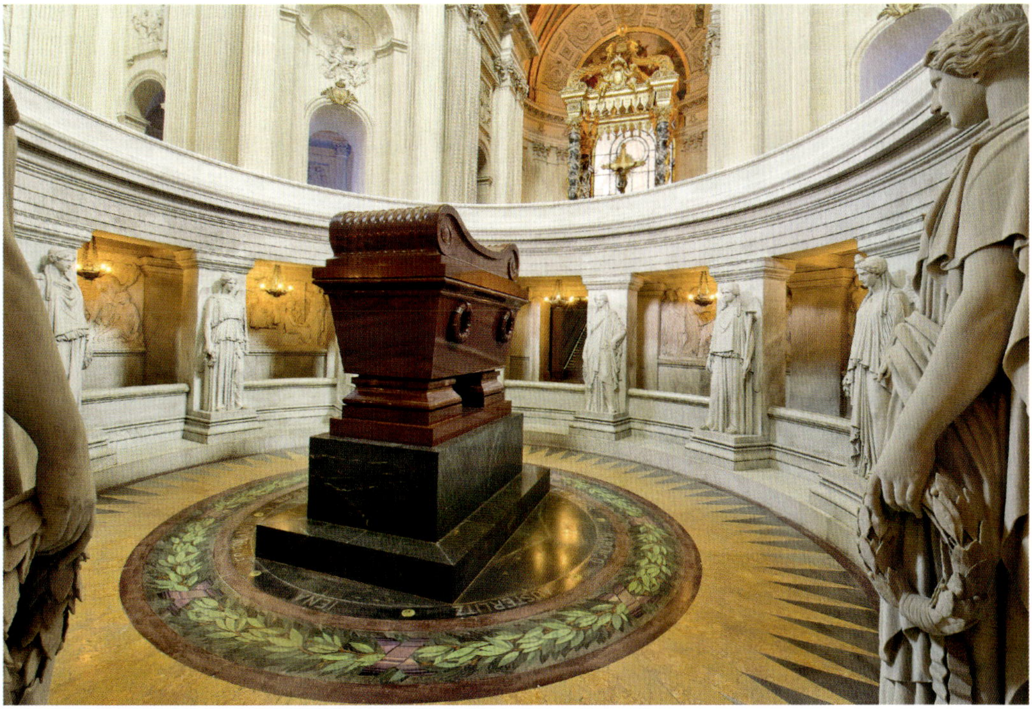

The bas-reliefs

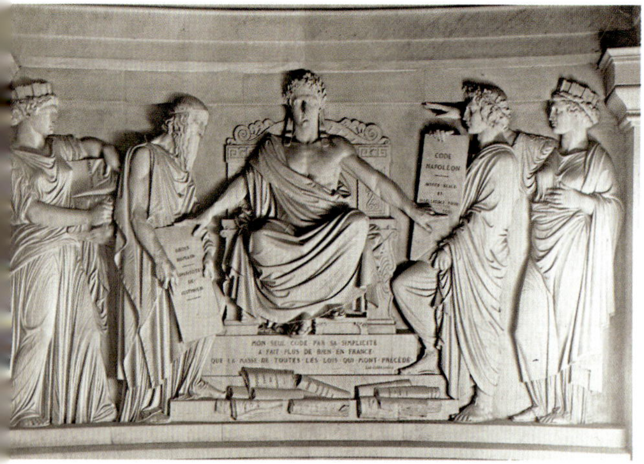

Pierre Charles Simart, *Creation of the French Civil Code (Napoleonic Code)*, Bas-relief, marble, 1846-1853. The principal legal compendium in France since 1804, the Civil Code has also been adopted by other countries.

In the circular gallery of the crypt, ten bas-reliefs in white marble evoke the major civil achievements of Napoleon Bonaparte. Works by the sculptor Pierre Charles Simart (1806-1857), these bas-reliefs are each 4.30 metres long and 2.60 metres high. Napoleon appears standing or sitting on a throne, dressed as a Roman emperor.

The bas-reliefs are divided into two groups. The first five compositions - civil peace, administrative centralisation, the State Council, the Civil Code and the Concordat - depict Bonaparte as the refounder of French society after the Revolution. For the other five - University, Court of Auditors, Industry and Commerce, Public Works and Legion of Honour - Napoleon appears as the guarantor of the functioning and prosperity of society.

The *cella* and the tomb of the Aiglon

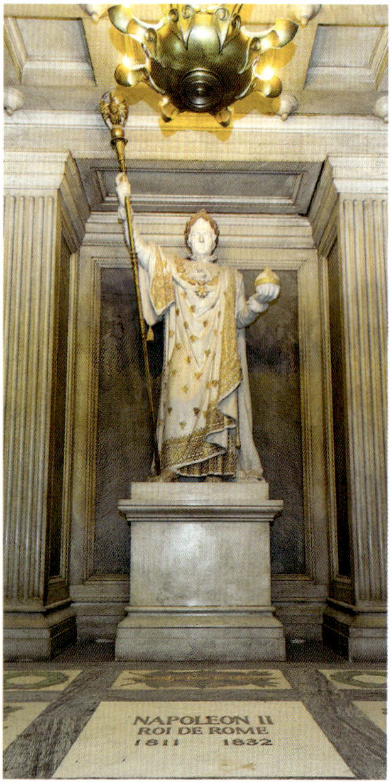

Cella of the Emperor's tomb: statue of Napoleon I dressed in coronation robes by Pierre-Charles Simart. The coat of the sovereign is dotted with bees, Napoleonic symbols. The tomb of Aiglon lies beneath the engraved floor plate.

In the middle of the gallery between the two sets of bas-reliefs, one room is furnished in the manner of a *cella* (central part of ancient temples). This small space, formerly called "room of the Sword", has long served as a shrine for the Emperor's personal property - sword of Austerlitz, bicorne hat from the Battle of Eylau, Grand Cordon of the Legion of Honour - now exhibited in the rooms of the Army Museum.

Fifty-six victories by Napoleon Bonaparte are listed on the walls of two side niches.

The niche to the rear is occupied by a statue in white Carrara marble. Created by Simart, it is 2.60 metres high and represents Napoleon in Coronation Robes.

At the foot of the statue, a slab bears the inscription "Napoleon II King of Rome, 1811-1832". Under this slab lies Aiglon, the only legitimate son of Napoleon I and his second wife, Marie Louise of Austria. Although he would never reign, Aiglon is often called Napoleon II. His ashes were transferred from Vienna to the Invalides by the Germans in 1940.

The Dome's other tombs

After the construction of Napoleon's tomb, other graves were installed in the Dome, definitively formalising its role as a necropolis.

Jérôme and Joseph Bonaparte

Under the Second Empire (1852-1870), the chapels near the entrance of the dome hosted the remains of Napoleon's two brothers. The youngest, Jérôme Bonaparte (1784-1860), was King of Westphalia - Northwest Germany - from 1807 to 1813 and governor of the Invalides from 1848 to 1852. Napoleon's elder brother, Joseph Bonaparte (1768-1844), was King of Spain from 1808 to 1813.

Foch and Lyautey

Historical events of the 20th century reactivated the Dome's role as a military pantheon.

In 1937, the tomb of the Supreme Commander of Allied Forces in the First World War, Ferdinand Foch (1851-1929), was completed by Paul Landowski (1875-1961) in the Chapelle St. Ambrose. In black bronze, the monument represents the remains of the Marshall borne by soldiers on laurels. On the bas-reliefs of the sarcophagus, the French army is depicted in all its diversity.

The Chapelle Saint-Grégoire hosts the tomb of Marshall Lyautey (1854-1934), administrator and peacemaker of Morocco where he was buried after his death. The transfer of his remains to France, decided in 1961 by General de Gaulle, symbolised decolonisation. The work of Albert Laprade (1883-1978), the tomb of Lyautey consists of a bronze coffin, one of whose inscriptions, written in Arabic, pays tribute to Morocco and its people.

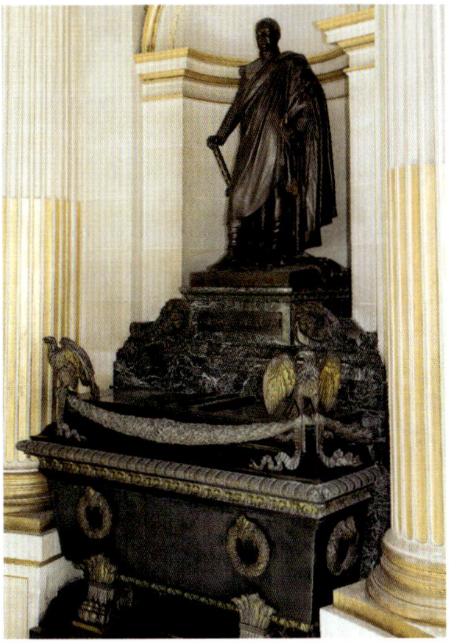

Tomb of Jérôme Bonaparte.

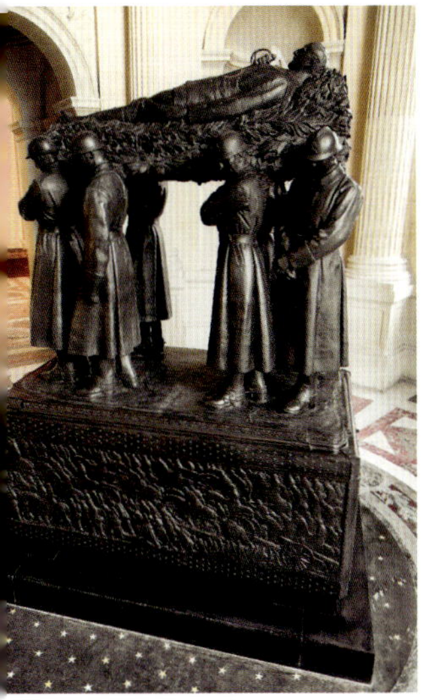

Tomb of Marshall Foch.

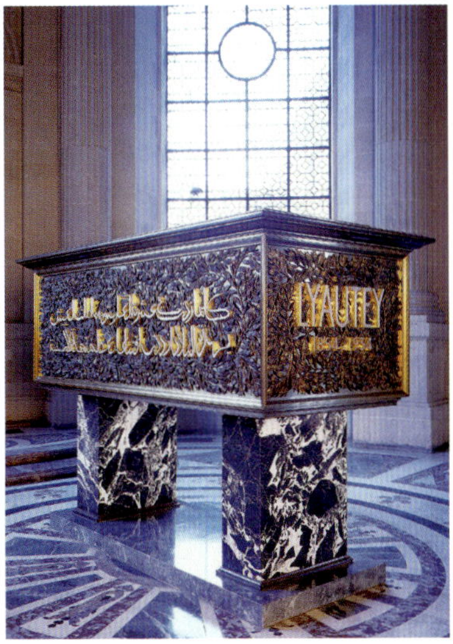

Tomb of Marshall Lyautey.

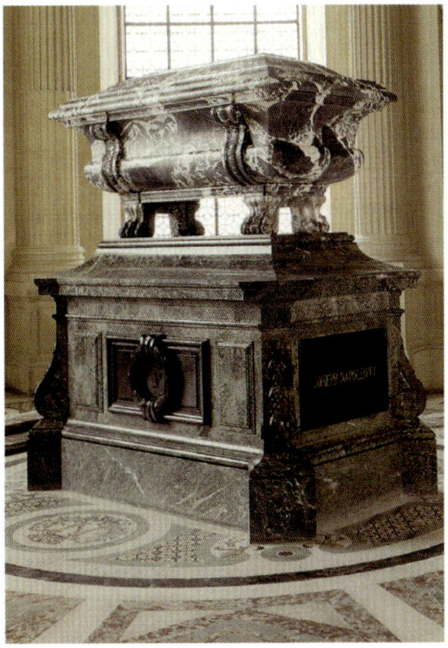

Tomb of Joseph Bonaparte.

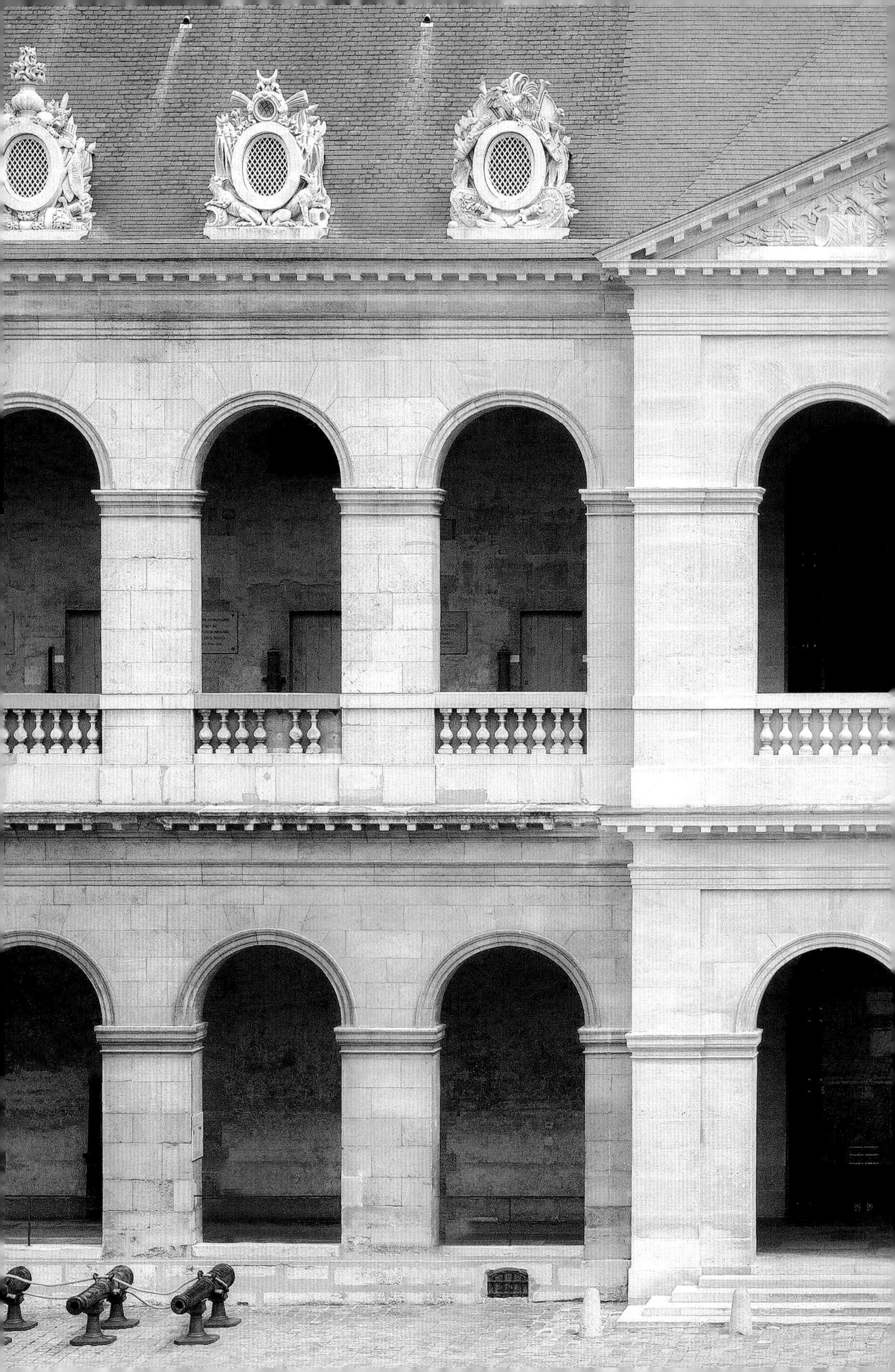

The Army Museum

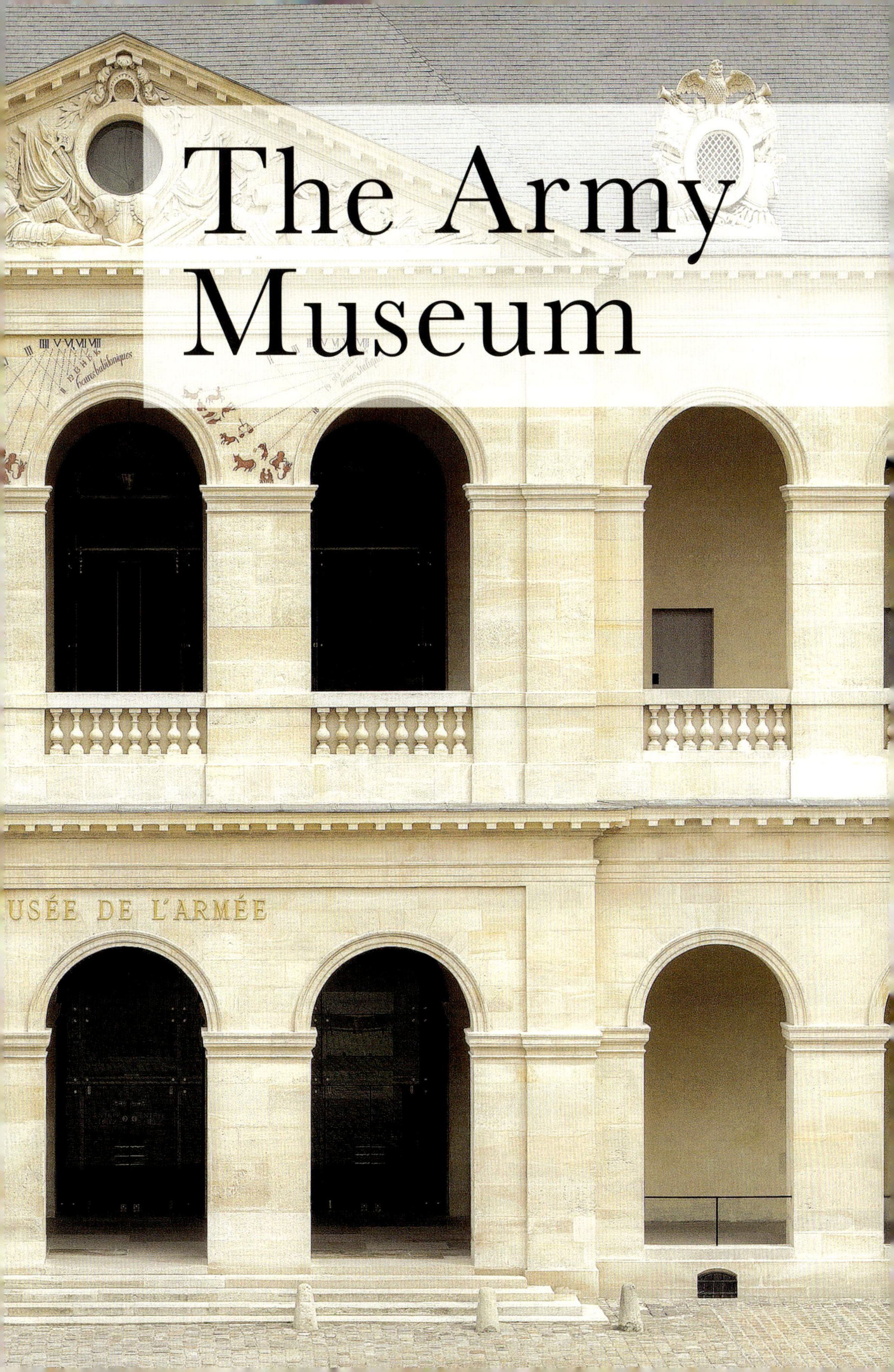

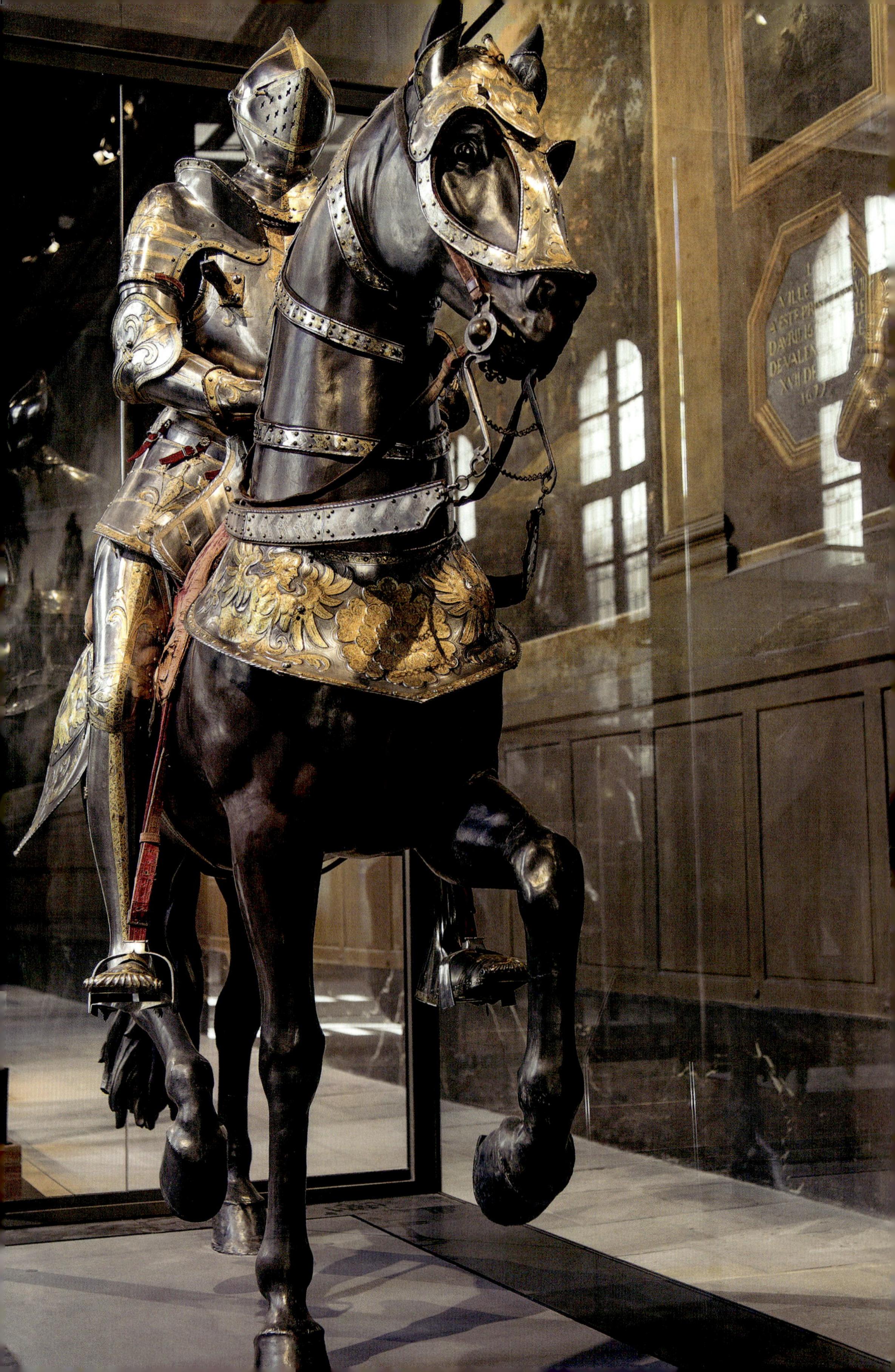

Ancient armour and arms from Saint Louis to Louis XIII

With 7,000 items, of which more than 1,500 on display, the collection of ancient armour and arms of the Army Museum is one of the three largest in the world, alongside those of Vienna and Madrid. Presented in the rooms of the West Wing of the Hôtel des Invalides, it retraces the evolution of warfare equipment from the 13th century through to the mid-17th century. It also includes several themed sections where opulent creations take centre stage, with the collections of the Crown being the most outstanding examples.

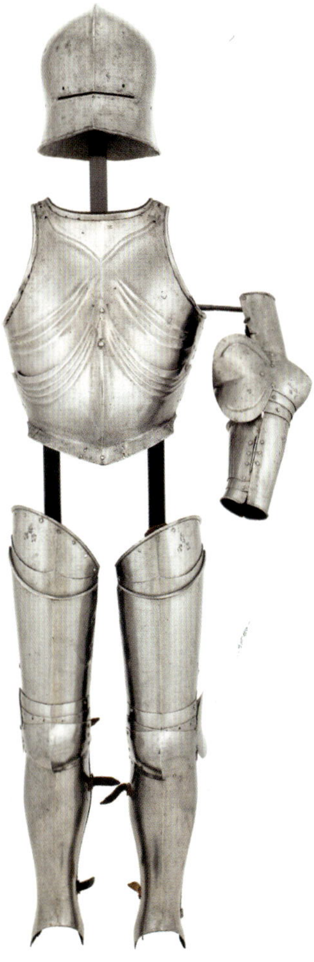

Arms and armour of war from the 13th to the 17th century

The objects in the old rooms reflect the history of the techniques and costumes of warfare from feudal times through to the death of Louis XIII.
The sword, which was the weapon of choice for the chivalry, is presented in its different typological variations between the 10th and 13th centuries, including remarkable examples of Viking swords. The 14th century saw the emergence of portable firearms and suits of armour, rigid metal protections worn over chainmail or replacing it entirely. The development of artillery is illustrated with a number of primitive pieces of ordnance and most notably the biggest bronze mortar bombs in the world (3,300 kilos) made in Rhodes at the end of the 15th century. This period was also marked by the spread of "harnois blanc", highly polished suits of armour with smooth, curved forms, a speciality of Milanese workshops.
During the wars of Italy (1494-1515), the Kingdom of France confronted the Empire of Charles V, represented by a wheel-lock

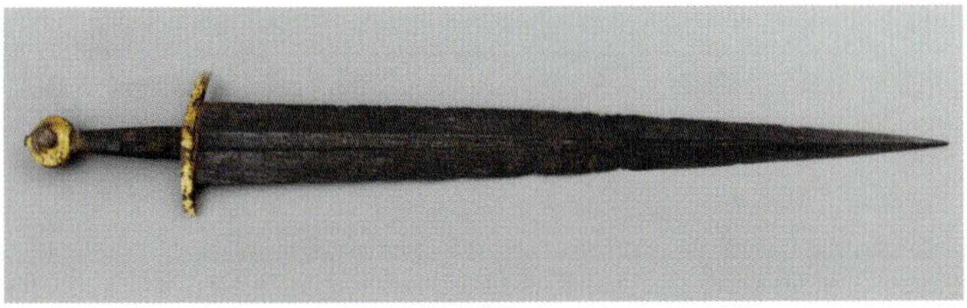

"Harnois blanc" suit of armour, of Milanese manufacture, 1480. Head protection: made in Innsbruck (?).

Sword, of French manufacture (?), 1350. The inscription "Clemency is the principal virtue" can be seen in Latin on the blade.

Left-hand page:
The Royal Room: the armour of François I.

pistol, not far from the sword of François I taken after the battle of Pavia (1525) and brought from Madrid on the orders of Napoleon in 1808.

The Franco-imperial rivalry, which dominated European politics until 1560, is also evoked through the blackened suit of armour of the Constable Anne de Montmorency, as well as by several suits of armour used by the Germanic lansquenets.

In its wars against the Habsburgs, France was allied with the Ottoman Empire. The latter's military power is recalled by Mamluk horse armour and a set of turban-helmets, including that of the Sultan Bajazet II, son of Mohammed II, the conqueror of Constantinople in 1453.

The Old Department also hosts objects related to the principal leaders of the religious wars which tore France apart in the second half of the 16th century. The armour of the Protestant Louis I of Condé is displayed opposite the extremely heavy armour of the Catholics Henri de Guise and his brother, the Duke of Mayenne.

Full armour continued to be worn during the first half of the 17th century, as evidenced by the stunning equestrian ensemble of Louis XIII. The wars waged by the King and his minister Richelieu are evoked in a painting by Laurent de La Hyre dating from around 1630.

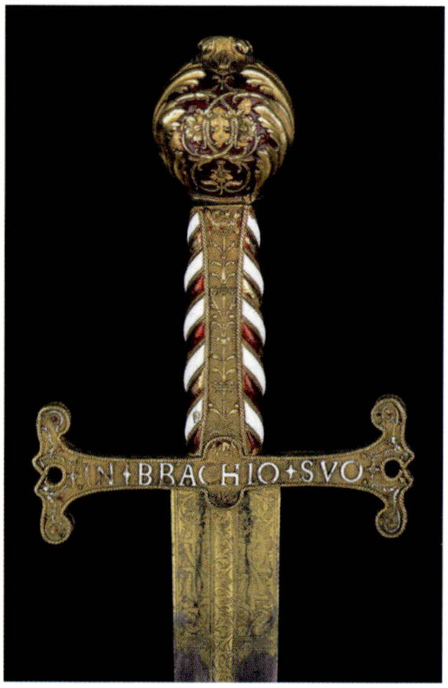

Sword of François I, of French manufacture (?), circa 1510-1515.
Blade: of Italian manufacture, circa 1480.
Iron, brass, gold, silver-gilt and enamel.

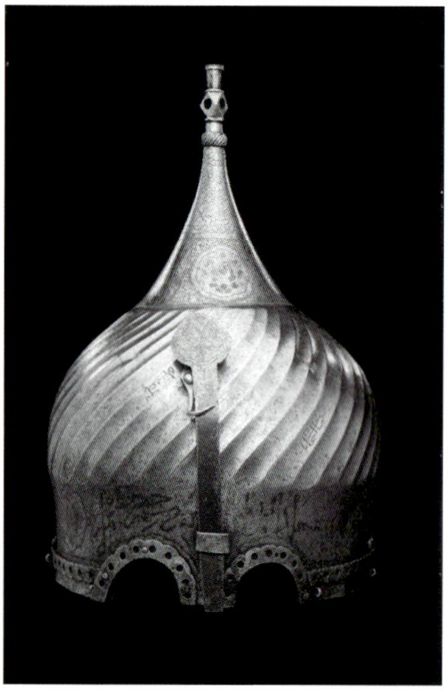

Turban-helmet, of Ottoman manufacture, circa 1480-1520.
This head protection has a movable nose guard.

The Arsenal Gallery

Being the visible storage area of the Old Department, the Arsenal Gallery allows visitors to discover some 2,500 offensive and defensive weapons from the 16th, 17th and 18th centuries.

The nine artillery pieces in bronze displayed in the corridor were made between the end of the 15th century and the beginning of the 16th century. They mostly originate from the island of Rhodes, ruled from 1309 to 1522 by the Hospitallers of St. John of Jerusalem.

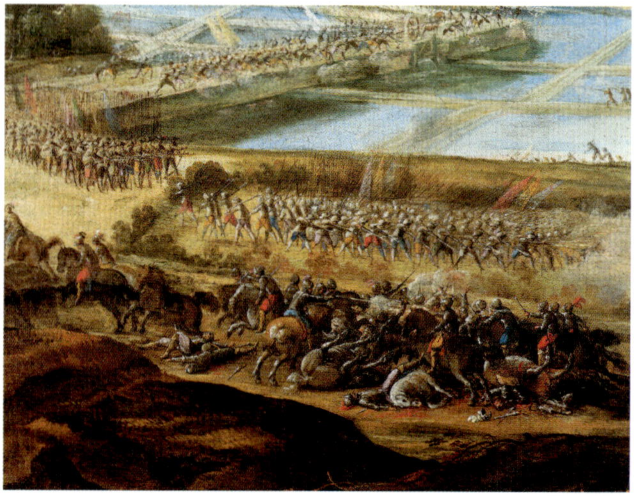

Laurent de La Hyre (1606-1656), *Defeat of the English at the Ile de Ré by the French army on 8 November 1627* (detail), circa 1630, oil on canvas, 1.12 x 2.10 m.

Hunting

An activity to obtain sustenance dating back to the very origins of man, hunting led to the emergence of specific weapons and instruments: swords, spears, tools for skinning game but also bows, crossbows, arquebuses with wheel locks and hand-held bayonets. The firearms illustrate the evolution of the hunting rifle from the 17th century through until today.

Jousting and tournaments

Following the example of hunting, jousting (one-to-one combats on foot or on horseback) and tournaments (combats between two troops of fighters) encouraged the development of specific protections tailored to the wide variety of these strictly codified sporting exercises which reached the height of their popularity in the 16th century.

The armour on display evokes jousting on foot in arenas, heavy German jousting (*Gestech* and *Rennen*), Italian-style jousting and equestrian festivities of the 17th century: ring or quintain jousting, equestrian displays, etc.

Several examples of garnitures, versatile units formed by armour and complementary pieces, are also presented. The most famous of these garnitures is the so-called "rose sheet" which owes its name to its decoration of serrated leaves and was made for the Emperor Maximilian II and his sons in 1571.

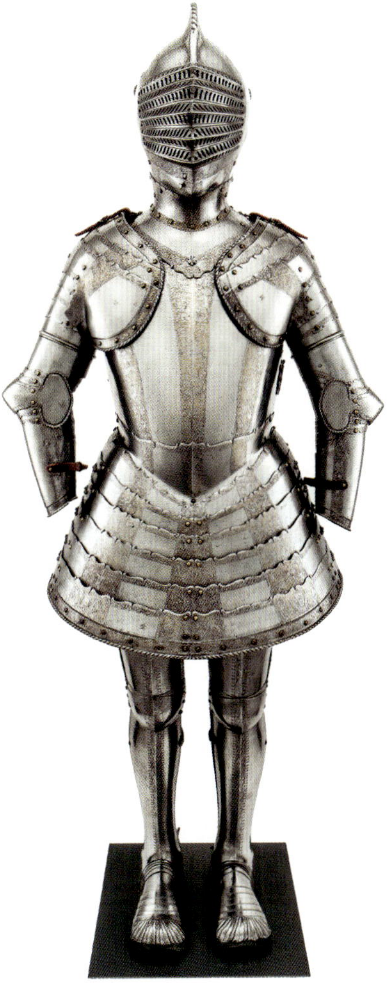

Tonlet armour for combats on foot in an arena, of Franco-Milanese manufacture, circa 1540-1550.
The tonlet is the long *braconnière* consisting of narrow plates down to the knees.
It compensates for the absence of a "lice" or barrier between participants who would use the sword or war hammer.

The major European workshops

The collections in the Europe room testify to the expertise of Italian, German and French armourers in the 16th and 17th centuries.

Cannon *Le Saint Gilles*, Lyon, 1507, bronze, l: 3 m, 2,032 kg.
Origin: Rhodes. This cannon belonged to the Hospitallers of St. John of Jerusalem.

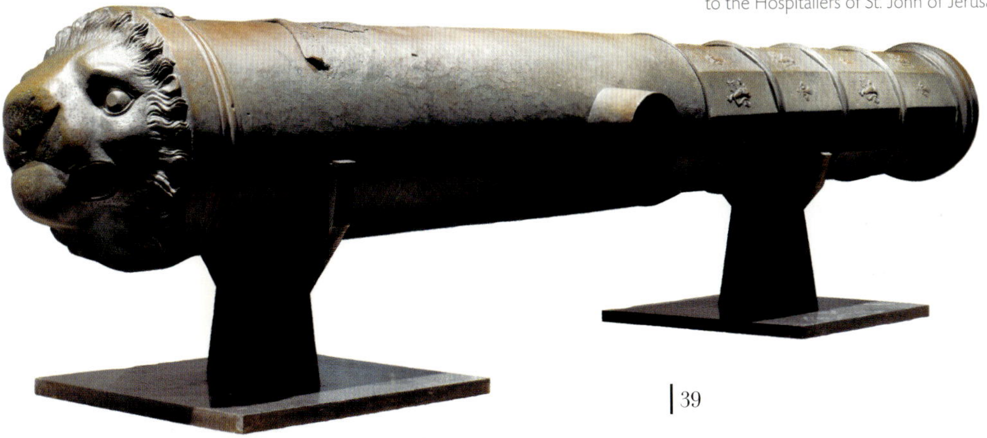

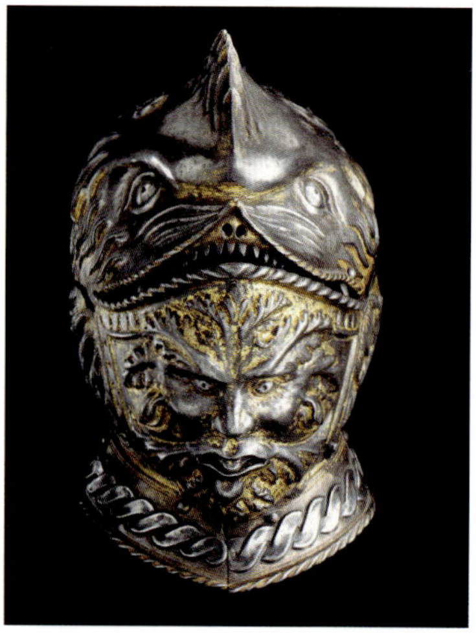

Burgonet helmet with griffin, of Milanese manufacture, circa 1540-1545.
The mannerist decoration combines a grotesque mask and a dragon's head.

The changing style of Italian armoury is reflected in the smooth shapes which can be seen in pieces by the Milanese artisan Niccolo Silva, dating from the early 16th century. Around 1530, this style gave way to that known as "Grande Maniera", mixing *repoussé* decorations and precious damascened inlays. After 1550, there was a return to a more sober decoration with etched vertical stripes, represented here by the pieces signed Pompeo della Cesa, who was active around 1580. Towards the end of the century, workshops in Brescia superseded those of Milan.
The German armoury centres of Nuremberg, Augsburg and Innsbruck also produced high quality pieces including "maximilienne" armour with distinctive ribbed surfaces; the gilded saddle and chamfer made for Ferdinand I in 1558 to mark the anniversary of the death of Charles V; or the spectacular equestrian armour of Otto Henry, Elector Palatine, made in 1531 by the Nuremberg armourer Hans Ringler.

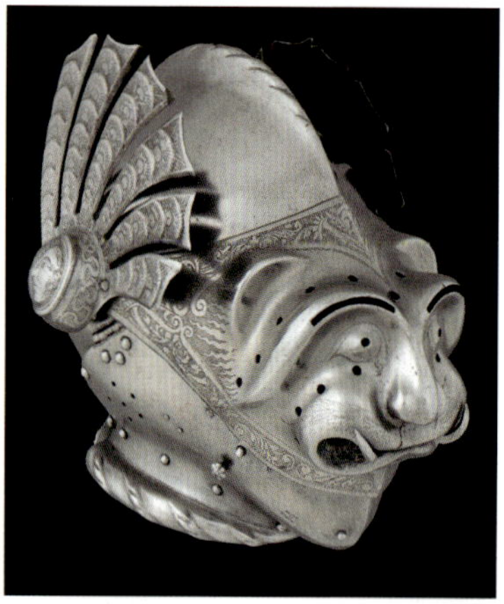

Armet belonging to Count Palatine Wolfgang, made in Innsbruck, circa 1520-1530.

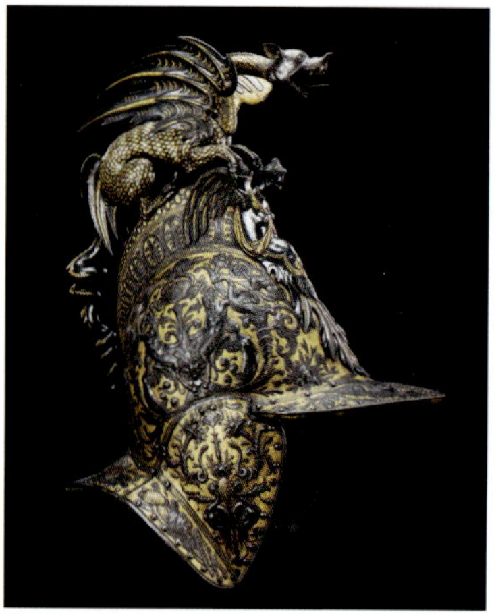

Burgonet helmet "à la chimère", a piece from the southern Netherlands, circa 1550-1660.

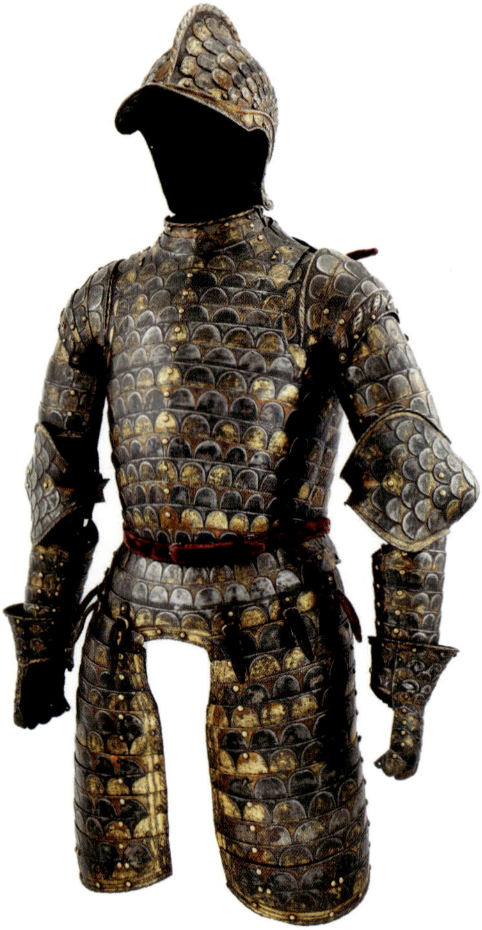

Ancient half armour, of Milanese manufacture (?), circa 1540.
The decoration of scales is inspired by *lorica squamata*, ancient body defences.

French output is present through the armour and arms of the Montmorency family, the only painted armour surviving, dating from the early 17th century and the beautiful ensemble "à la chimère", characteristic of the French Mannerist style.
As a complement to the adjoining Europe room, a small side room offers a selection of output from major French, Italian, Spanish and Dutch sword and arquebus makers in the 16th, 17th and 18th centuries.

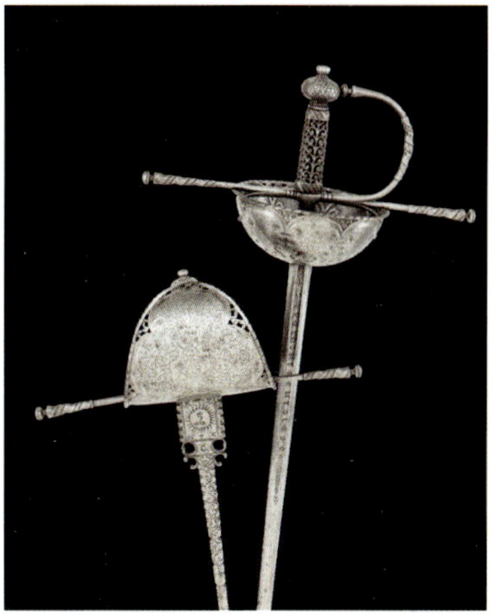

Oriental collections

Part of the museum's collection consists of armour, swords, daggers and guns from Ottoman, Indian, Chinese, Japanese and Indonesian warrior cultures. The most remarkable piece is undoubtedly the war dress of the Chinese Emperor Ch'ien Lung (1736-1796), donated to the museum by Napoleon III after the 1860 campaign. Most of the Japanese pieces were donated by collectors and enthusiasts in the last quarter of the 19th century, such as the large collection of ceremonial helmets (*Kabuto*) on display. Other oriental objects found their way to the museum as part of the Crown's old collections.

A "Taza" rapier and its left-handed dagger, Spain, circa 1650.

Iro Iro Domaru no Yoroi type armour, of Japanese manufacture, circa 1600, steel, brass, leather and silk.

Military parade dress of the Emperor Ch'ien Lung, of Chinese creation, circa 1758.

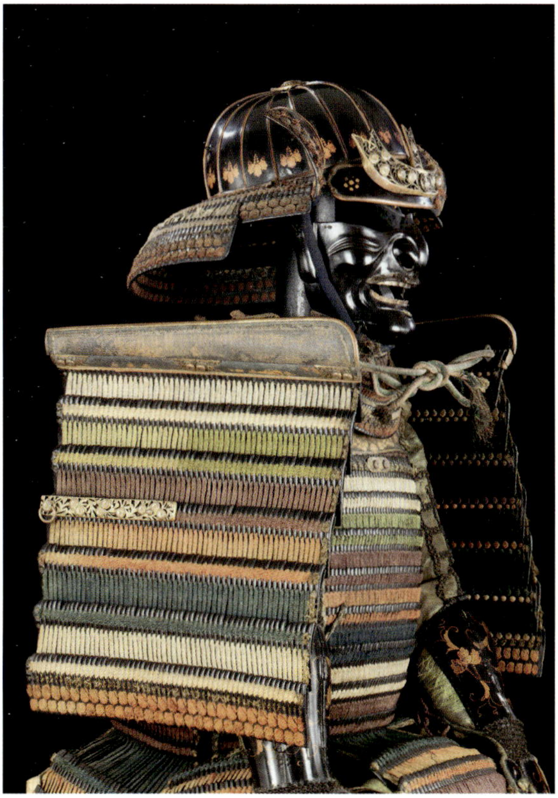

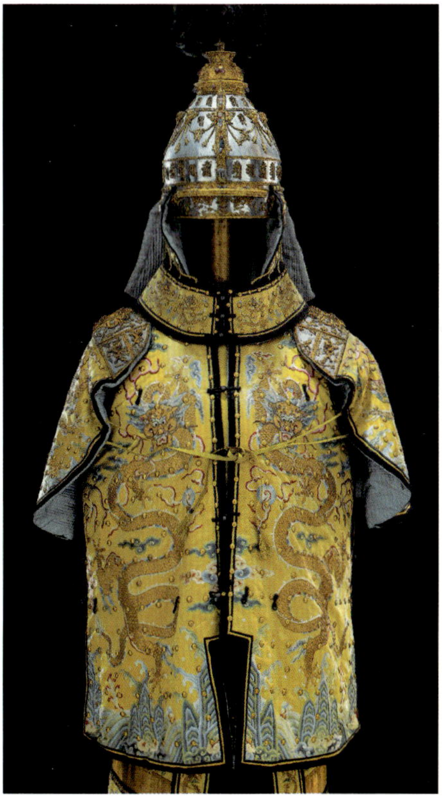

Collections of the Crown

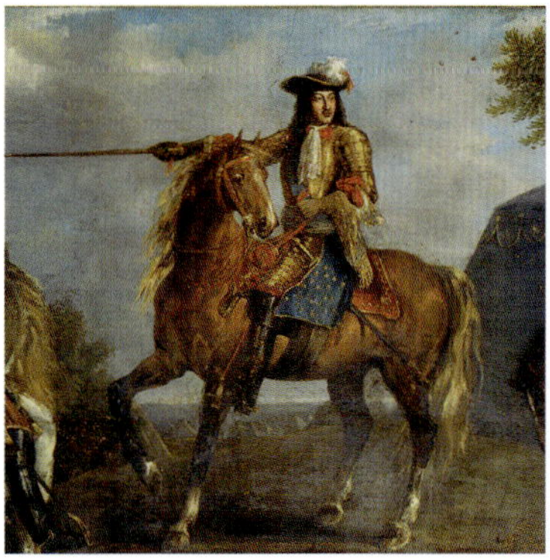

Joseph Parrocel, *The conquests of King Louis the Great in the years 1676, 1677 and 1678*, circa 1679-1680, oil on plaster and stone, detail of the decoration of the Royal Room, former refectory of the Hôtel.

Up until the French Revolution, most of the royal armour and arms were kept in the Crown's Furniture Repository installed in the palace built by Gabriel, now the Hôtel de la Marine, located alongside the current site of the Place de la Concorde. What remains is on display in the Royal Room, a former refectory, whose wall paintings depict military scenes from the Dutch War (1672-1679). These works by Joseph Parrocel (1646-1704) were restored in 2005 with the support of the Crédit Industriel et Commercial (CIC). The other pieces in the Royal Room are from the principal French (Sedan, Chantilly) and foreign royal armouries. Some are of oriental origin. Before its transfer to Paris in 1806, the grand equestrian armour of François I (see p. 36), created in 1539, formed part of the cabinet of arms of the Archduke Ferdinand of Tyrol at Ambras Castle (Austria). Two masterpieces come to us from the workshop of the Negrolis, Milanese master armourers: "The lion armour" *repoussé* work was most probably commissioned by François I and the fully inlaid "armour of the Dauphin" for his son, the future Henry II. The popularity enjoyed by the Italian workshops at the court of France is illustrated by other stunning pieces such as the mace belonging to Henry II and the German crossbow (firing clay pellet) of his wife Catherine de Medici. It was for one of their sons, Charles IX, that may have been made "the armour to Mars and Victory," whose *repoussé* ornamentation is inspired by the Franco-Flemish Mannerist style. Several arms and standing combat armour evoke Henri IV, of whom the museum owns a portrait by Marin Le Bourgeois, both painter to the King and a renowned gunsmith.

Among the sovereigns who have most enriched the old collections of the Crown, pride of place unquestionably goes to Louis XIII. Fascinated since childhood by war-related

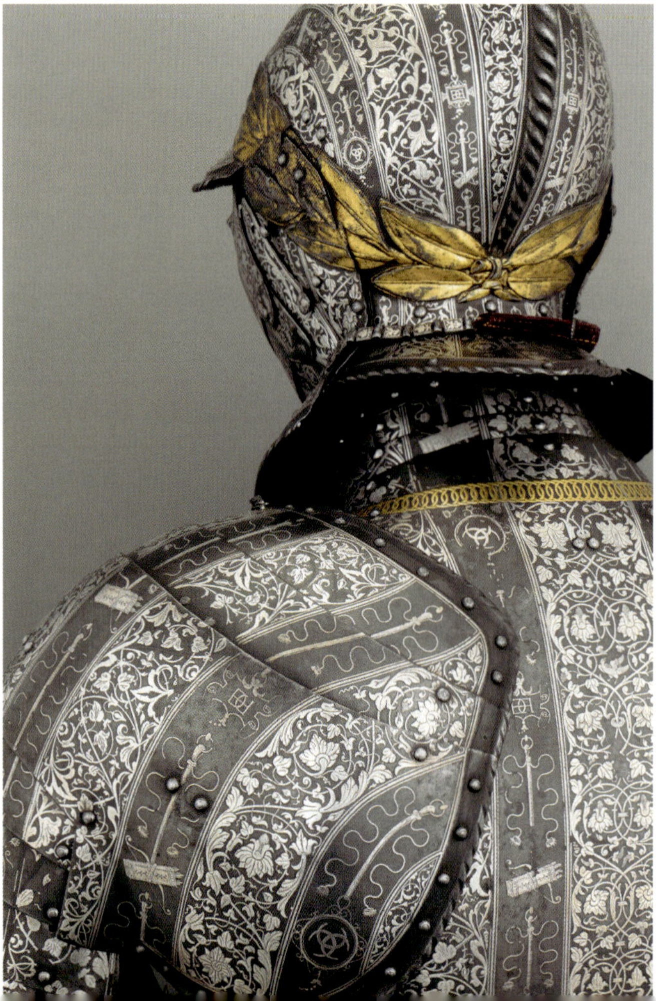

Francesco Negroli and his brothers, the armour of the dauphin Henry, the future Henry II, Milan, circa 1540, detail. Of an exceptional quality and beauty, inlaid silver decorations embellish the intertwined crescents of the Valois, the letter "H" (Henry) associated with the "C" of his wife Catherine de Medici; the bows and quivers may evoke Diane de Poitiers, the prince's mistress.

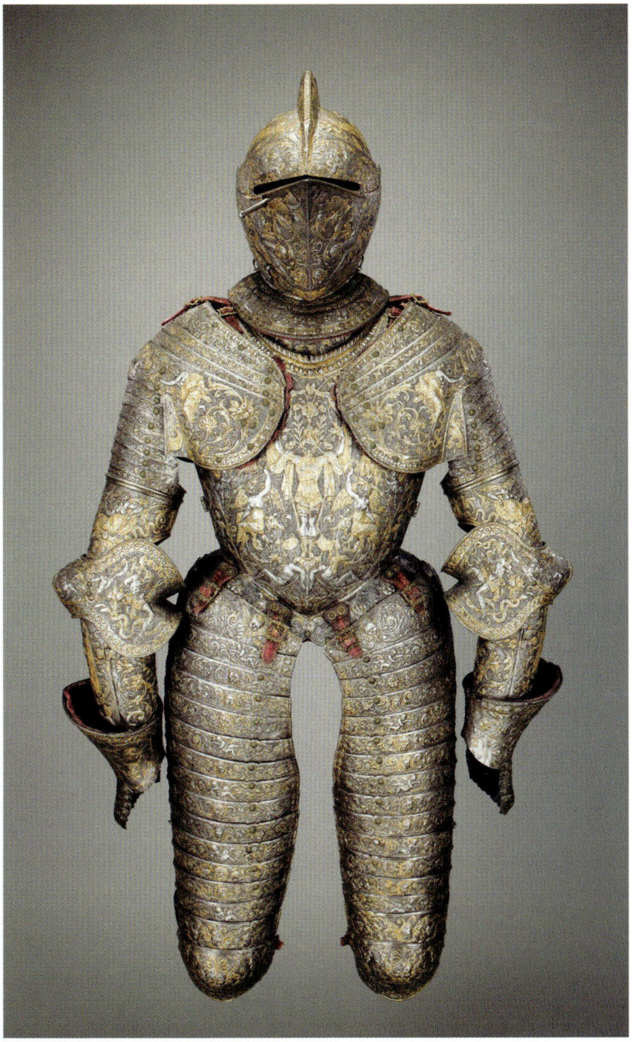

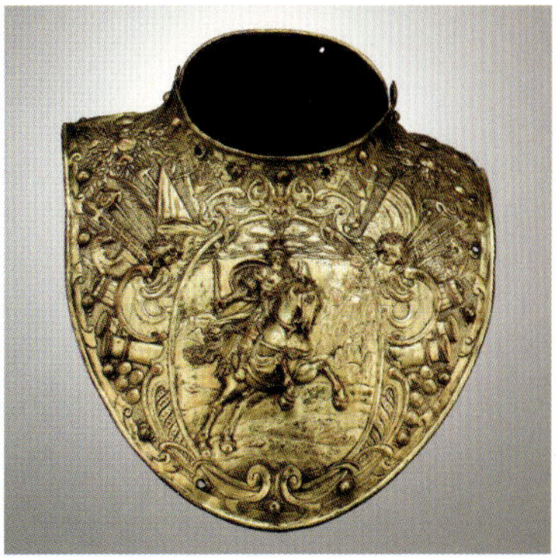

Neck guard thought to have belonged to Louis XIII, French work, circa 1620-1630, *repoussé* copper and gilded.
The decoration shows Louis XIII on horseback.

"Armour to Mars and Victory," of French manufacture, circa 1565-1570.
The centre of the breastplate of this sumptuous armour, perhaps intended for Charles IX, is decorated with a representation of the god Mars.

objects, the son and successor of Henry IV built up an extraordinary cabinet of arms with a particular abundance of armour and guns. The latter are characterised by their high quality and innovative systems. They are supplemented by pieces of remarkable finesse from Brescia, Germany and Holland.

The armour of Louis XIV, offered in 1668 by the Republic of Venice, is of poor blacksmithing quality although this is offset by the exquisite engraved decoration. The oriental pieces which surround it – Ottoman armour, round shields and quivers as well as Japanese armour - were probably diplomatic gifts for the court of France.

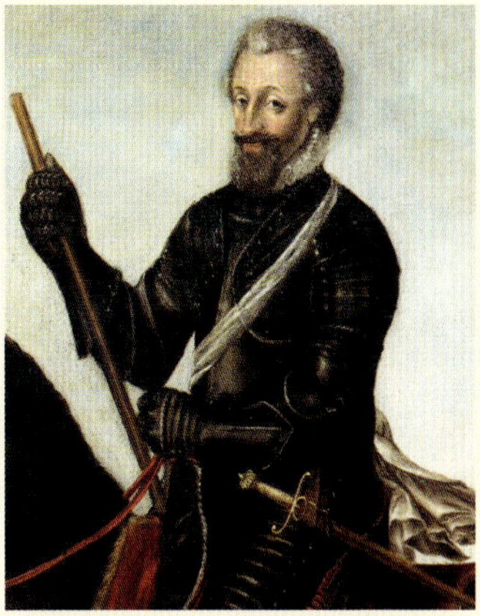

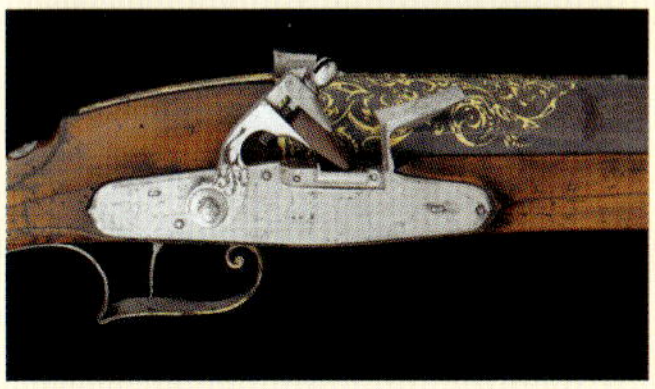

Marin Le Bourgeois, painter and gunsmith

This equestrian portrait of Henry IV (after 1594, oil on wood panel, detail) and this high-powered rifle (Lisieux, circa 1620) demonstrate the multiple talents of Marin Le Bourgeois (circa 1560-1634), artisan serving Louis XIII and supposed inventor of the flintlock (visible on the rifle).

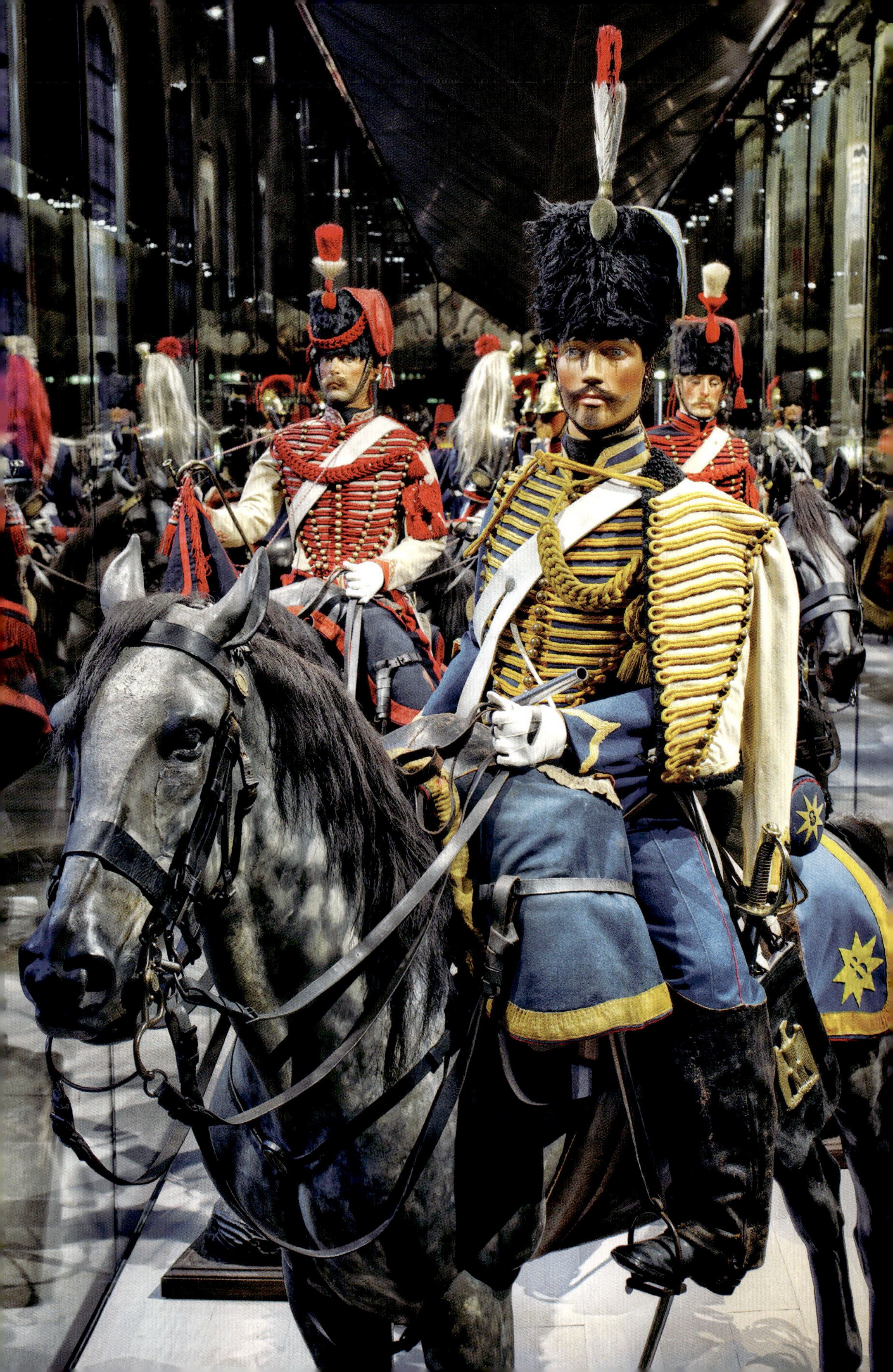

Modern collections from Louis XIV to Napoleon III

Located in the East wing of the Hôtel, the modern rooms trace the history of the French army from 1643 to the Franco-Prussian war of 1870. In the former rooms of disabled soldiers, more than 2,000 items are on display and placed in context, thanks to a host of multimedia devices.
This circuit is completed by two themed ensembles: on the ground floor, the Vauban room, a former refectory now dedicated to the history of the cavalry from 1799 to 1870, and on the first floor, rooms devoted to musical instruments, artillery models and military figurines.

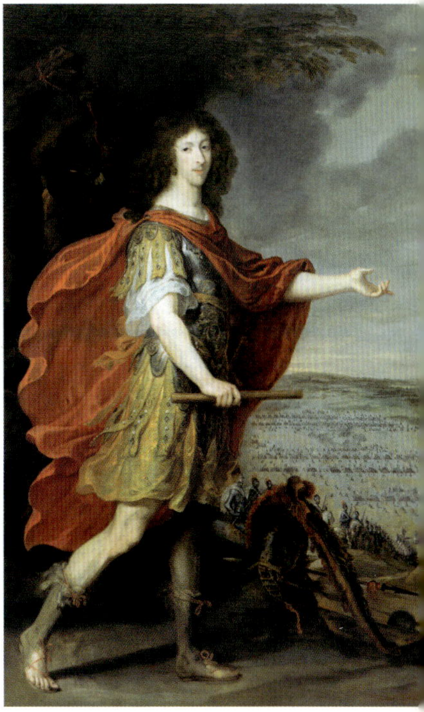

Juste d'Egmont *Louis II de Bourbon, Duc d'Enghien, in front of the battlefield of Rocroi* 1645, oil on canvas, 2.46 x 1.63 m.

Infantry rifle, 1717 model, factory of Saint-Etienne. This rifle is the first French official model.

Left-hand page
Vauban room.

The king's army (1643-1792)

The defeat of the Spanish army at Rocroi on 19 May 1643, just five days after the death of Louis XIII, inaugurated an era of French dominance in Europe. The author of this success, the Duc d'Enghien, future Grand Condé (1621-1686), is represented in a classical style portrait by Juste d'Egmont (1601-1674), which marks the beginning of the visit.
During the long reign of Louis XIV (1643-1715), the army was reorganised, regulated and controlled by the royal power. The uniform, the bayonet and the rifle were adopted. Outfits, emblems and portraits illustrate the role of the royal household, composed of elite troops for the protection of the sovereign. The museum also exhibits some personal effects of Maréchal de Turenne (cannonball and back of breastplate) and evokes the figure of Vauban, a specialist in siege warfare. The daily life of the troops is presented through recruitment, equipment, music and emblems.

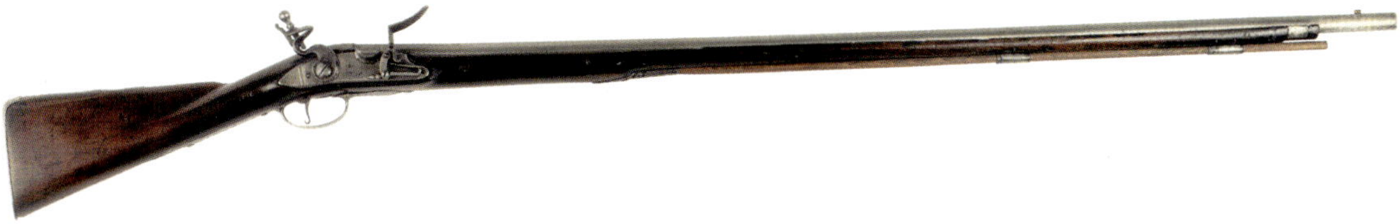

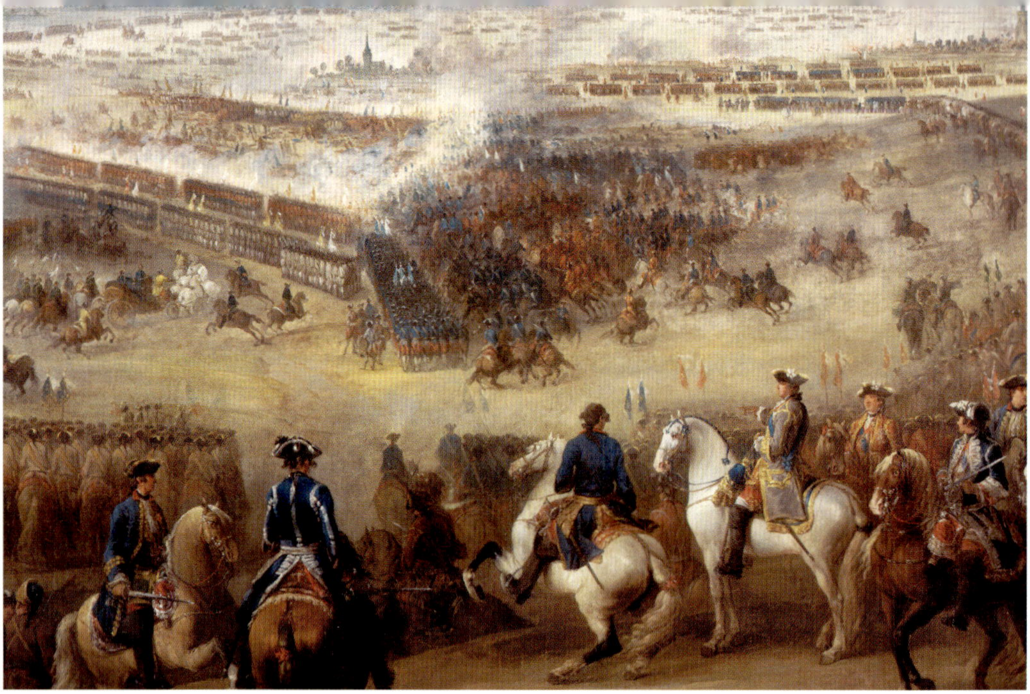

Pierre Lenfant (1704-1787), *The Battle of Fontenoy*, 11 May 1745, circa 1750-1760, oil on canvas, 2.49 x 2.72 m, detail.
Fontenoy depicted France's greatest victory during the War of the Austrian Succession (1740-1748). In the foreground, King Louis XV and his son witness the actions of the French cavalry and infantry against the column of the British and Hanoverians.

In the 18th century, efforts to regulate the army continued with the adoption of the 1717 rifle and 1786 uniform. The Franco-British rivalry characterises the conflicts of the second half of the century: the War of the Austrian Succession and the War of Seven Years then American Independence.

The Army of the Nation (1792-1804)

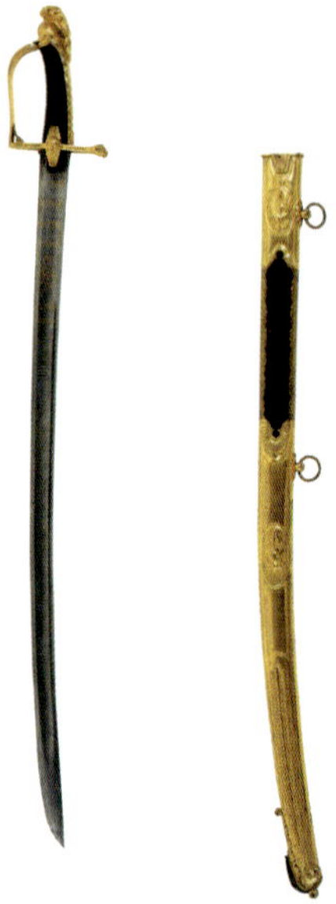

Sabre probably presented to General Hoche in reward for the pacification of the Vendee.

On 20 April 1792, Revolutionary France declared war on Austria, soon joined by Prussia and then Great Britain the following year. Undermined by undisciplined troops and the mass emigration of officers, the French army suffered serious setbacks. It also had to suppress internal opposition such as the uprising in the Vendee. Faced with these perils, the revolutionary authorities responded vigorously by increasing the ranks of serving men - the Army had 750,000 men in 1794 compared with 150,000 in 1791 - and renewing the officer corps. These measures paved the way for the victories of Valmy, Jemappes and Fleurus, which saved the Revolution.

From this transformed army emerged the figure of General Bonaparte. Born in Corsica in 1769, he enjoyed considerable prestige after his victories in Italy, as evidenced by the keys to Milan, a city taken in 1796. The expedition to Egypt, evoked by the harnesses of the Mamluks defeated at the Battle of the Pyramids (21 July 1798), enhanced the reputation of the young general. Following the coup d'état of 18 Brumaire Year VIII, which gave rise to the manufacture of memorial swords, Bonaparte assumed the title of First Consul. The peace concluded with Austria (1801) and Great Britain (1802) and the increased powers conferred on him by the status of Consul for Life, left him a free hand to restore domestic order and create long-lasting institutions: prefects, the Banque de France, high schools, Legion of Honour, Civil Code.

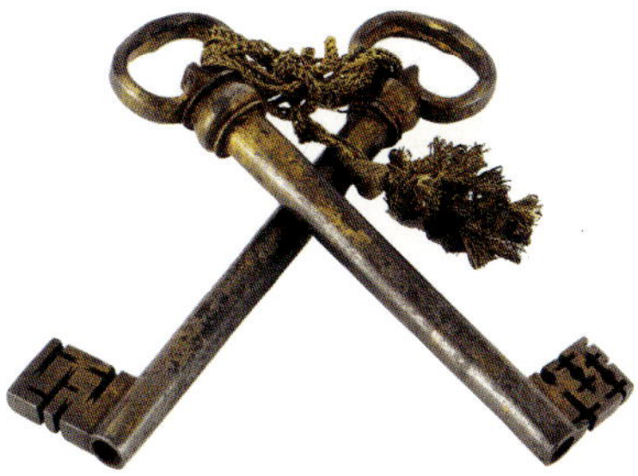

Keys to the castle of Milan surrendered to the French army on 29 June 1796.

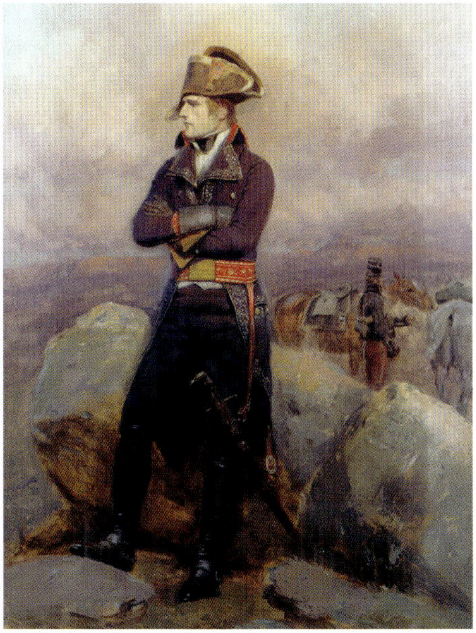

Édouard Detaille (1848-1912), *General Bonaparte*, circa 1900, oil on canvas, 67 x 47.5 cm.
A century later, the famous military artist, Edouard Detaille, chose for this portrait the figure of a young general of the Republic, less known than that of the triumphant Emperor.

The army of the Emperor (1804-1815)

Proclaimed Emperor by the Senate in May 1804, Napoleon Bonaparte arranged for his coronation to be held on 2 December at Notre Dame Cathedral in Paris. The room dedicated to this event is dominated by the large portrait by Jean Auguste Dominique Ingres, *Napoleon I on the imperial throne*, of archaic style. Other portraits and several ceremonial outfits evoke the creation of a court and reinstatement of the title of Marshal, abolished by the Revolution. The Sovereign's security was ensured by the Imperial Guard, a fully-fledged reserve army whose elite was formed by foot grenadiers, wearing the famous bearskin helmets. Military matters absorbed the new regime, which was soon confronted by a new anti-French coalition made up of Great Britain, Russia and Austria. These latter two powers suffered a heavy defeat by Napoleon's forces on 2 December 1805 at Austerlitz in Moravia. The strategy of the battle is presented using an animated relief map. The victory of Austerlitz and those of Jena (1806), Eylau and Friedland (1807), allowed Napoleon to dominate Europe. The role of the various weapons of the Great Army developed in the course of a campaign or a particular battle,

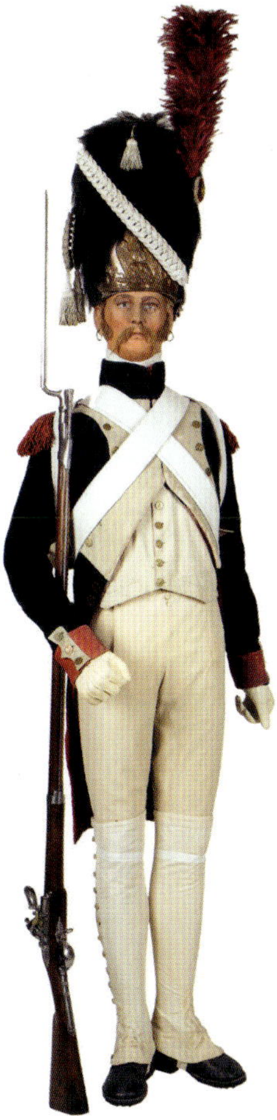

Grenadier of the Imperial Guard in full dress, circa 1804-1815.

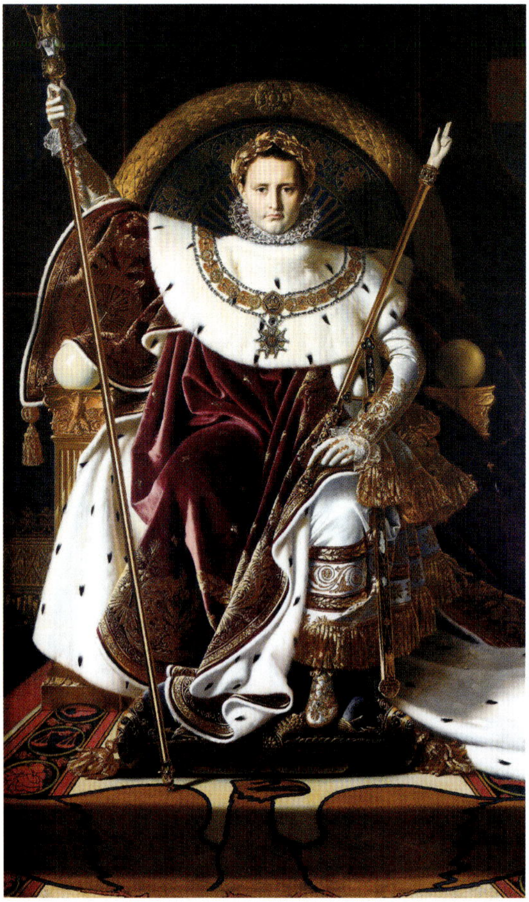

as for the artillery at Wagram in 1809. The life of the Emperor on a military campaign is itself the subject of a room where, behind the black hat and austere grey frock coat, the folding furniture is a reminder that warfare required its proponents to be continually on the move.

From 1808, the conquest of Spain, which evolved into guerrilla warfare, caused the first breach in the Empire. However, its subsequent collapse was the result of Napoleon's intervention in Russia in 1812. The strategy of retreat adopted by the Tsar and his generals eventually exhausted the Napoleonic troops, although they still managed to take Moscow. The November retreat, in temperatures of minus 30, decimated the Great Army, reduced to 50,000 men out of an initial deployment of 560,000. Reconstructed in 1813, it was wiped out in Germany once more by Russia and its allies (Prussia, Austria and Sweden).

The allies entered Paris on 31 March 1814. The retrospective painting by Paul Delaroche, *Napoléon I at Fontainebleau,* captures the dramatic atmosphere of this day for the legendary figure also known as the Eagle, who had retreated to Fontainebleau and was forced to abdicate on 6 April 1814. Facing the painting, the museum

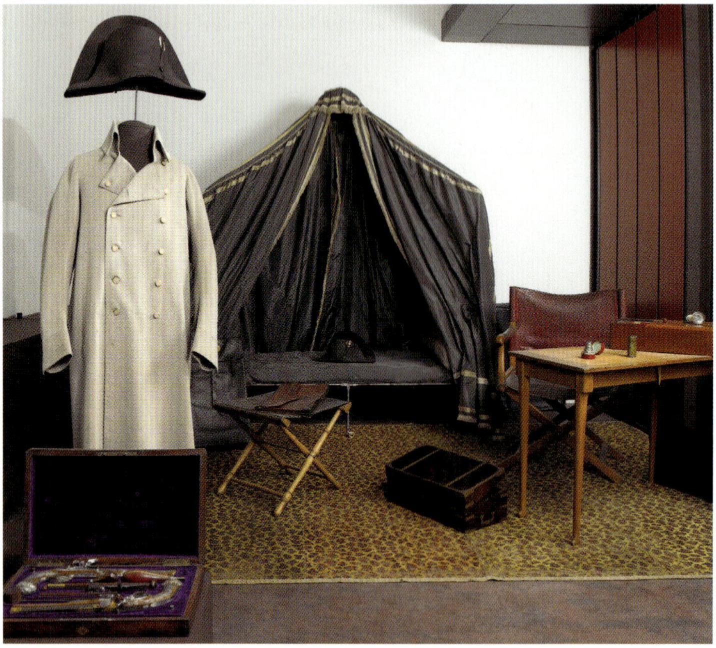

Jean Auguste Dominique Ingres (1780-1867), *Napoleon I on the imperial throne,* 1806, oil on canvas, 2.59 x 1.62 m.

Campaign clothing and furniture of Napoleon I.

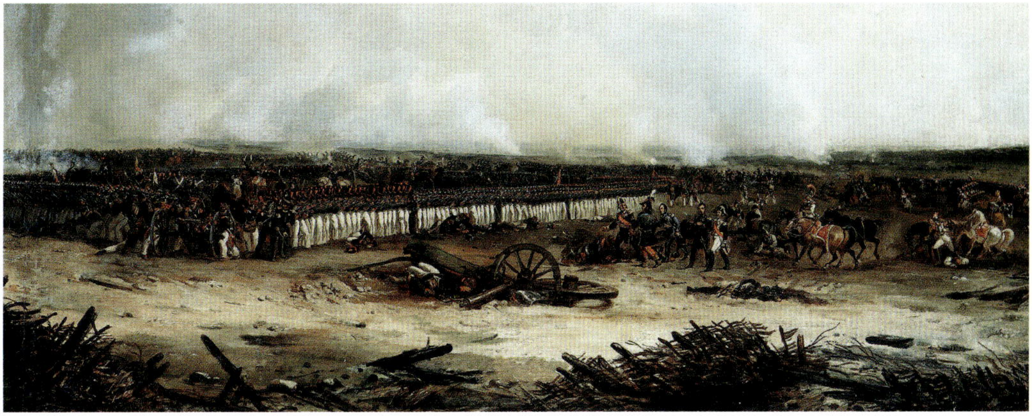

displays the Farewell flags, kissed by Napoleon before his departure for the island of Elba. France became a monarchy once more, ruled by the Bourbon Louis XVIII, brother of the late King Louis XVI. Returned to power during the Hundred Days (March-June 1815), Napoleon was finally defeated by the British and Prussians at Waterloo, on 18 June 1815. The breastplate of the rifleman Fauveau, pierced by a cannonball, vividly expresses the violence of battle. After his second abdication, Napoleon was exiled to the British island of St. Helena (see p. 29). The new borders of the European states were drawn up by the Congress of Vienna (1814-1815).

Jean Charles Langlois, sketch or model of *Panorama of the Battle of Borodino*, 1835-1838, oil on canvas, 0.745 x 6.95 m, detail.
Due to the strategy of retreat adopted by the Tsar, the Battle of Borodino (7 September 1812) was one of the few major military confrontations of the Russian campaign.

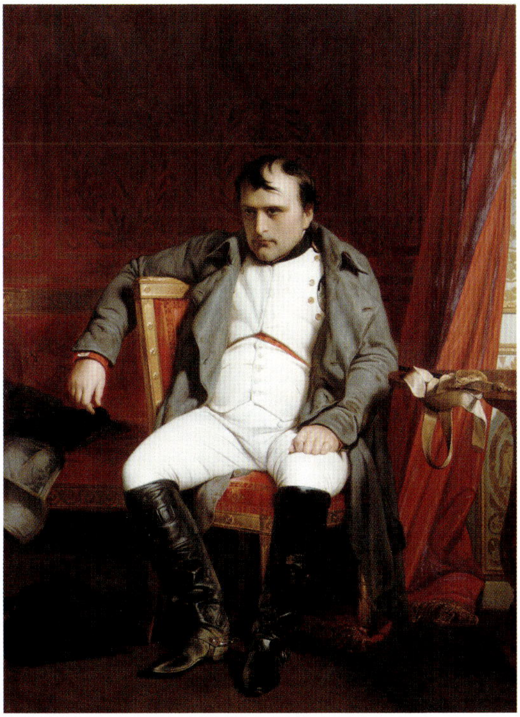

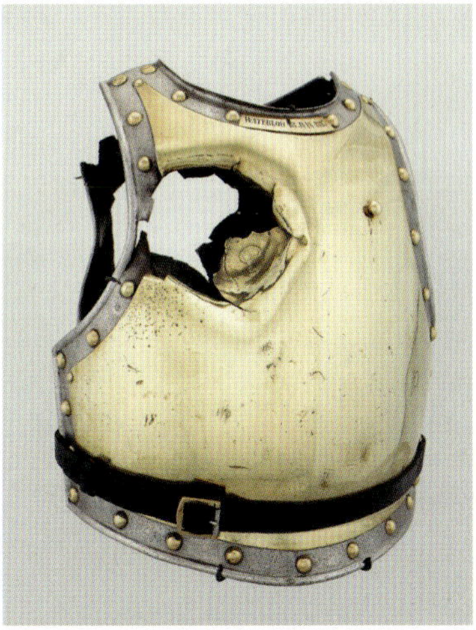

Breastplate of the rifleman Fauveau killed by a cannonball at the Battle of Waterloo in 1815.

Hippolyte Delaroche known as Paul Delaroche (1797-1856), *Napoleon I Fontainebleau, 31 March 1814*, 1840, oil on canvas, 1.81 x 1.37 m.
Representing Napoleon defeated and alone in a room in the château of Fontainebleau, this work replaces the image of the conqueror with that of the romantic hero.

The army of 1815-1870

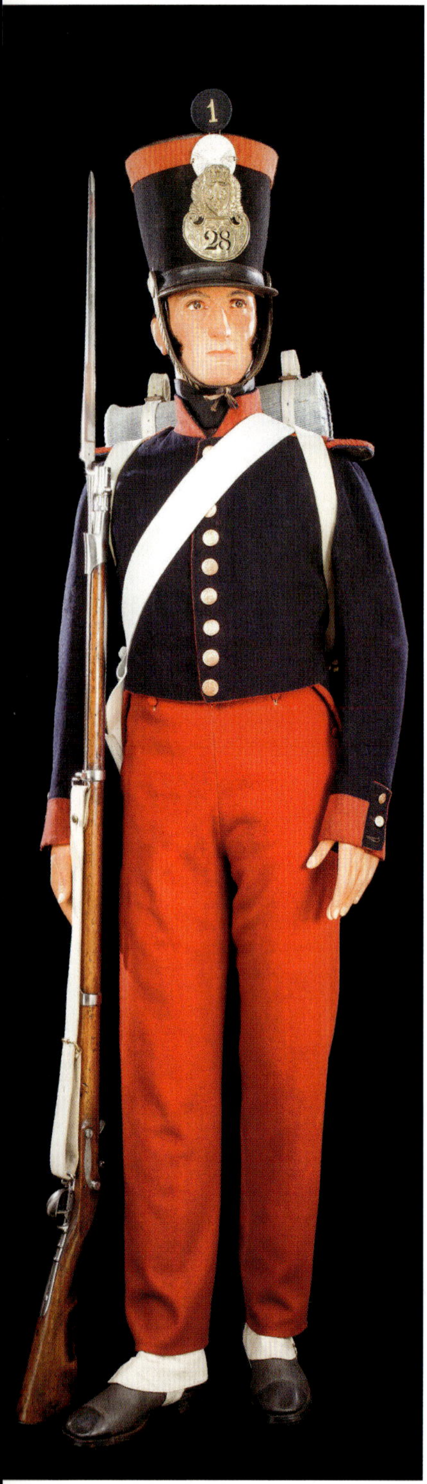

Fusilier of the 28th regiment of the Infantry line, circa 1829-1830. Introduced in 1829, the bright red trousers were worn until 1914.

From the end of the Hundred Days through to the 1870 war, the army served the successive political regimes in France: Restoration (1815-1830), the July Monarchy (1830-1848), the Second Republic (1848-1852) and the Second Empire (1852-1870). Suspected of Bonapartism by the Bourbons, after their reign the military fulfilled missions to maintain order in a repressive manner. Under the Second Empire, it took an active part in the prestigious events of the regime, such as the cavalry manoeuvres of the Chalons encampment.

Conscription, random selection and the replacement system regulated recruitment. The status of officers was created in 1834. In terms of uniforms and equipment, the bright red trousers were adopted in 1829, while from 1840, several technological revolutions transformed the soldier's musket: the percussion lock, the rifled barrel and breech loading gave rise to the Chassepot model of 1866.

Overseas, the key event of the period was the conquest of Algeria, symbolised by the keys to the city of Algiers, taken by the French on 5 July 1830. In Europe, France tried to regain its status as a great power in the campaigns of Spain (1823), Morea (1828-1829), Belgium (1831-1832), Rome (1849-1850) Crimea (1854-1856) and Italy (1859). During the war against Prussia and its German allies (1870-1871), the forces of Napoleon III were surrounded at Sedan and the enemy besieged Paris, where the Commune uprising broke out. After the defeat, Alsace and northern Lorraine were annexed by the new German Empire.

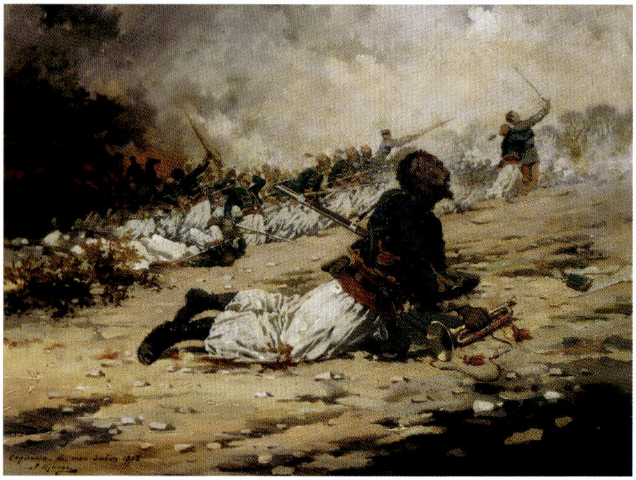

Jules Monge (1855-1934), *Clairon de Turcos injured, 6 August 1870*, circa 1888, oil on canvas, 0.44 x 0.6 m. The Turcos (Algerian infantry) involved in the fighting in 1870 against the Prussians and their allies.

The rooms of musical instruments, artillery models and military figurines

Closely linked to the chronology of the modern period, important themed collections are presented on the first floor of the east wing, in a series of rooms spread over more than 300 square metres.

The selection of primarily wind and percussion instruments on display highlights the traditional role of military music, namely, to transmit orders, set the rhythm for marching and boost the fighting spirit of the troops, but also its popular appeal and its function as a political educator. Its place in the army-nation relationship and exchanges with civil music, illustrated by the concert programme of the Army Museum, are also covered.

The museum's collection of artillery models is one of the most important in the world, both in terms of quantity and quality. The majority of the pieces presented in the rooms demonstrate the technical development of artillery whose memory they preserve while recording progress from the Renaissance through to the 19th century. Some models, however, are princely *objets d'art* and fulfilled the function of honorary gifts.

The third space relates the history of the military figurine through a range of 5,000 pieces, out of approximately 200,000 kept by the Army Museum. Originally intended for collectors and children, the figurines exhibited, in card or paper, in two or three dimensions, embody the richness and diversity of the collection. Countries and units represented, manufacturing and large collections are among the main themes of the visit proposed.

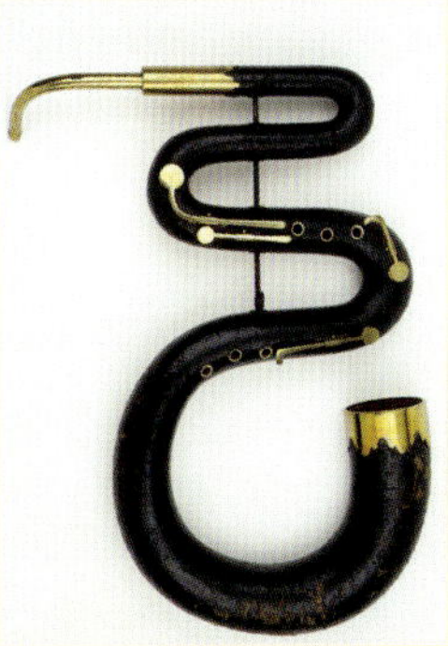

Francis Pretty, military serpent (bass wind instrument), 19th century, wood covered with leather, brass.

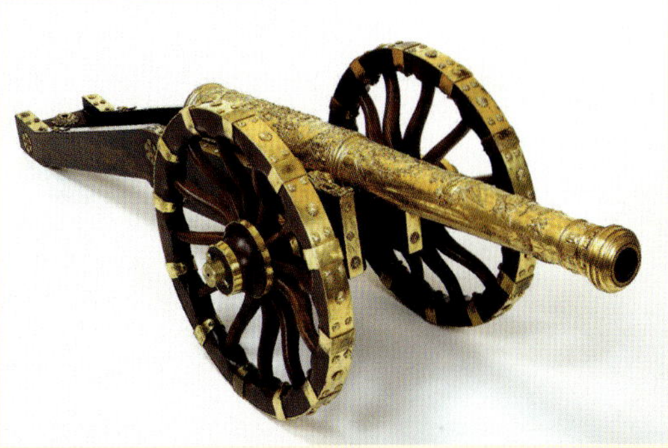

Laurent Ballard, the so-called Franche-Comté cannon, 1676, ormolu, gilded brass, fruitwood, 0.36 x 1.26 m, offered by the parliament of Franche-Comté to Louis XIV.

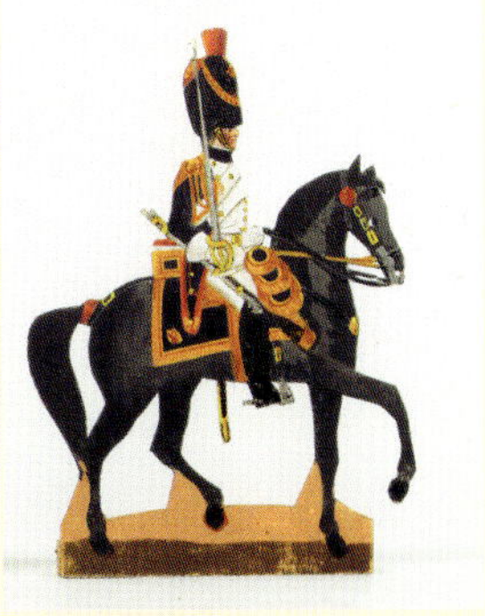

Wurtz-Pees families, Imperial Guard, regiment of Mounted Grenadiers (1804-1815), Strasbourg, 1825-1855, paper figurine in watercolour mounted on cardboard, h. 0.17 m.

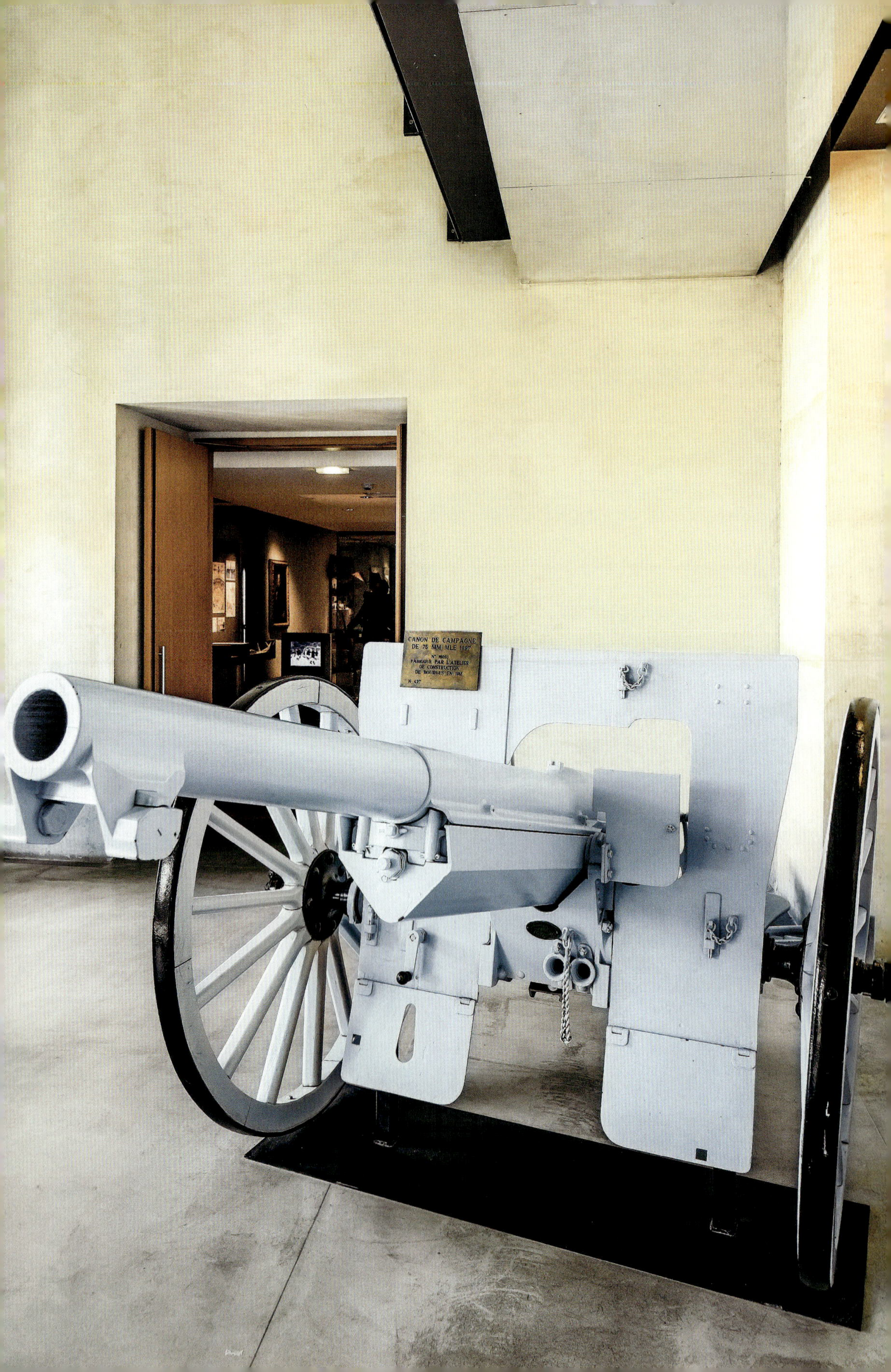
CANON DE CAMPAGNE
DE 75 MM MLE 1897
FABRIQUE PAR L'ATELIER
DE CONSTRUCTION
DE BOURGES EN
N 427

The two World Wars: 1871-1945

With over 3,000 items spread across 3,500 square metres, the circuit devoted to the two World Wars presents the military history of France from 1871 to 1945. The two major conflicts of the 20th century, 1914-1918 and 1939-1945, constitute important stages. The presentation follows a logical timeline and attaches considerable importance to the European - dominated by Franco-German antagonism - and world context of the period.

In search of "Revenge" (1871-1914)

Military paintings of the 1880s, evoked by the works of Alphonse de Neuville (1835-1885) and Edouard Detaille (1848-1912), preserve the painful memory of the defeat of 1870-1871. With a view to taking revenge against the German Empire, the Third Republic began rebuilding the army through significant measures such as the introduction of military service which was made compulsory and universal in stages between 1872 and 1905. For public opinion, the army was the subject of a national consensus which the Dreyfus Affair (1894-1906) failed to diminish. Armaments were upgraded with the adoption of the Lebel 8-mm repeating rifle and development of the 75-mm rapid-fire field gun.

Meanwhile, to compensate for its isolation in Europe, France resumed its process of colonial expansion overseas. Personal items belonging to the Commander Marchand, as well as Generals Gallieni and Lyautey illustrate the role of the army in the conquest and administration of the new African, Madagascan and Indochinese territories.

Left-hand page:
The 75-mm field gun model 1897.

Alphonse de Neuville and Edouard Detaille
The bottom of the cartridge pouch, fragment of *Panorama of the Battle of Rezonville, 16 August 1870*, 1882,
oil on canvas, 293 x 259 cm.

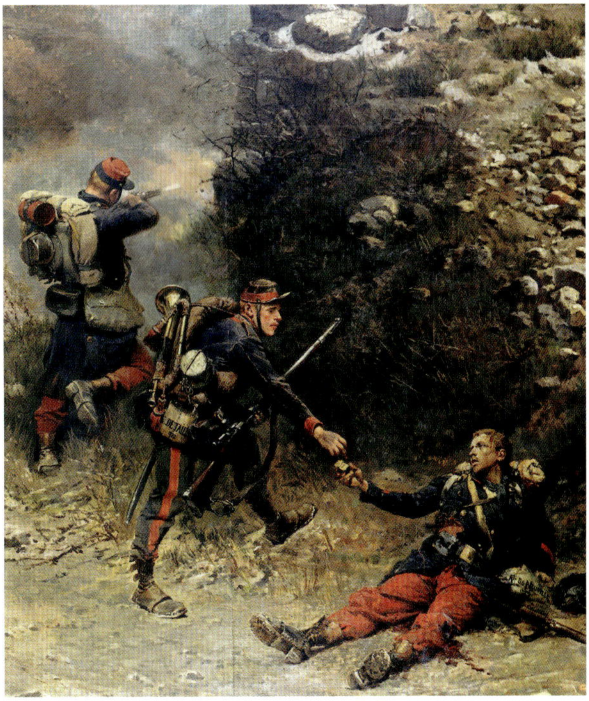

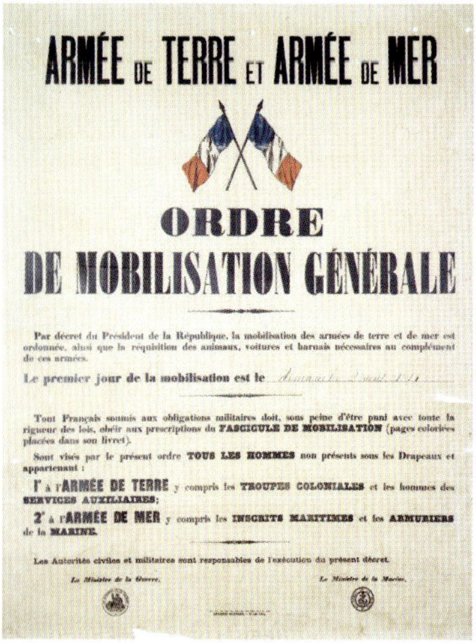
ARMÉE DE TERRE ET ARMÉE DE MER

ORDRE
DE MOBILISATION GÉNÉRALE

Par décret du Président de la République, la mobilisation des armées de terre et de mer est ordonnée, ainsi que la réquisition des animaux, voitures et harnais nécessaires au complément de ces armées.

Le premier jour de la mobilisation est le

Tout Français soumis aux obligations militaires doit, sous peine d'être puni avec toute la rigueur des lois, obéir aux prescriptions du FASCICULE DE MOBILISATION (pages coloriées placées dans son livret).

Sont visés par le présent ordre TOUS LES HOMMES non présents sous les Drapeaux et appartenant :

1° à l'ARMÉE DE TERRE y compris les TROUPES COLONIALES et les hommes des SERVICES AUXILIAIRES;

2° à l'ARMÉE DE MER y compris les INSCRITS MARITIMES et les ARMURIERS de la MARINE.

Les Autorités civiles et militaires sont responsables de l'exécution du présent décret.

Le Ministre de la Guerre. Le Ministre de la Marine.

General mobilisation order of 2 August 1914, poster, National Printing Office.

A First World War soldier from the French 60th Infantry Regiment in battle dress, circa 1916-1917.

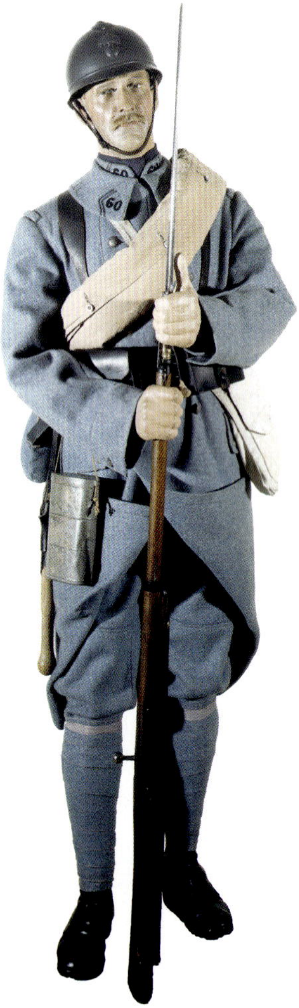

World War I (1914-1918)

The crisis following the assassination in Sarajevo (28 June 1914) took just a few weeks to trigger the outbreak of war in Europe. Allied with Russia, France decreed a general mobilisation on 2 August while Germany declared war on 3 August. Great Britain in turn entered the conflict after the invasion of Belgium by German forces, a manoeuvre which meant it was able to threaten Paris.

The defence of the capital was the focus of the great French offensive of the Marne in September 1914. The vehicle on display in the museum recalls the symbolic role of Parisian taxis during this battle, following which the German troops were forced to retreat. The uniforms presented alongside illustrate the general appearance of the fighters at the beginning of the Great War (French bright red trousers, German spiked helmet).

In the autumn of 1914, the war of movement gave way to the war of trenches dug by the soldiers on both sides to protect themselves against the deadly effects of machine guns and shells. These buried lines were effectively defended by thick barbed wire. The model of a trench built in captivity by a French officer gives us an insight into the appalling conditions of daily life at the front: exposure to cold and mud, overcrowding, boredom, poor hygiene, separation from family. All of which undermined the morale of soldiers.

The weapons of the war of position are collected together on a podium surrounded by display cases presenting periscope rifles, machine guns, grenades, mortars and shells, whose fragments could pierce steel. The use of poisoned gas in chemical warfare required appropriate protection, from a simple compress to a full mask. Changes in methods of combat led to changes in uniforms, transformed by the abandonment of bright red trousers and the adoption of the sky blue colour, the Adrian helmet and leggings.

The production of these weapons and equipment led to unprecedented industrial mobilisation, which involved 400,000 women in 1918. Financial participation by civilians was encouraged by large-scale war bond poster campaigns disseminating propaganda messages, characteristic of the first total war in history. The involvement of colonial empires also gave it a global dimension. France mobilised the 800,000 veterans and workers of its colonies (especially African).

A series of uniforms (British Italian, Russian, Romanian and Serbian) reminds us of the existence of other fronts along the Italian-Austrian border, in eastern Europe, the Balkans and in Ottoman Palestine.

1917 saw the United States enter the war alongside the Allies, represented by the flag of the first American volunteers offered to the Army Museum on 4 July 1917. The withdrawal of Russia

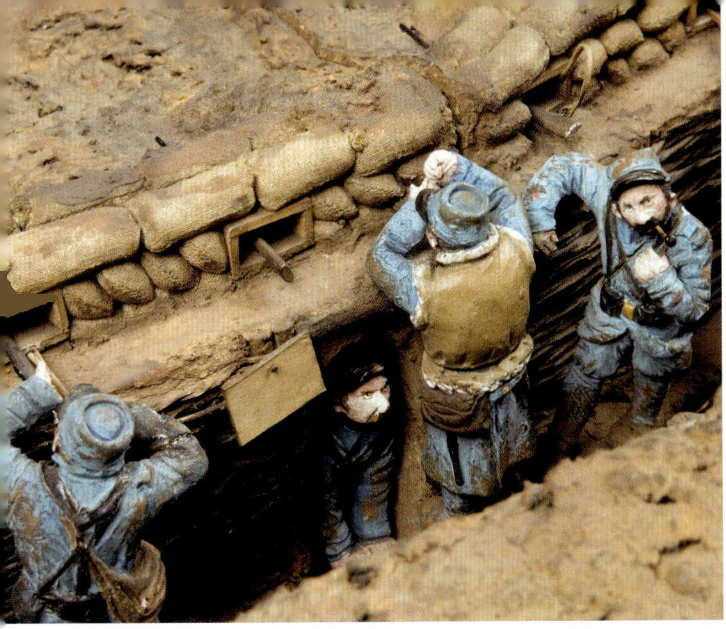

Scale model of a trench, begun in 1915 by Captain Reboud during his captivity in Germany, scale: 1:20, detail.

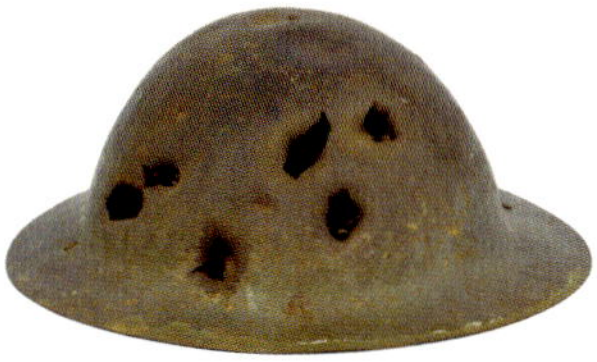

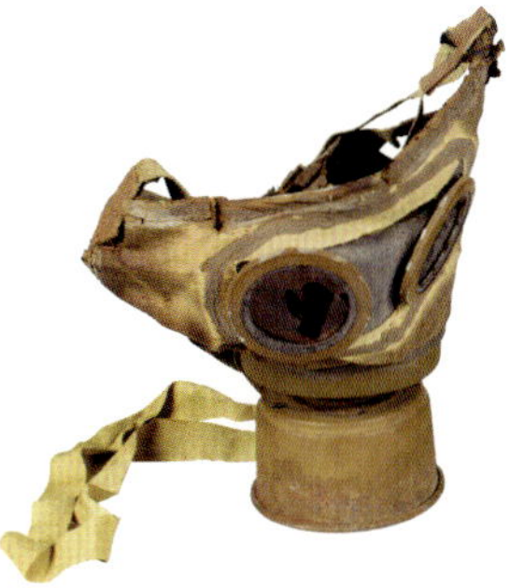

Top:
British helmet pierced by shrapnel, circa 1916.

Bottom:
Gas mask termed special breathing apparatus, France, 1917 model.

was a consequence of the Bolshevik revolution. The growing involvement of the British Dominions in the conflict (Canada, Australia and New Zealand) is highlighted by military uniforms from these countries. In France, 1917 was also a challenging year for soldiers, marked by bouts of poor morale and mutinies.
1918 saw the return of a certain mobility of fronts, made possible by the increased use of tanks and aircraft by the Allies. Under the combined effects of these new weapons, the presence of 2 million American soldiers in Europe and the decision to make

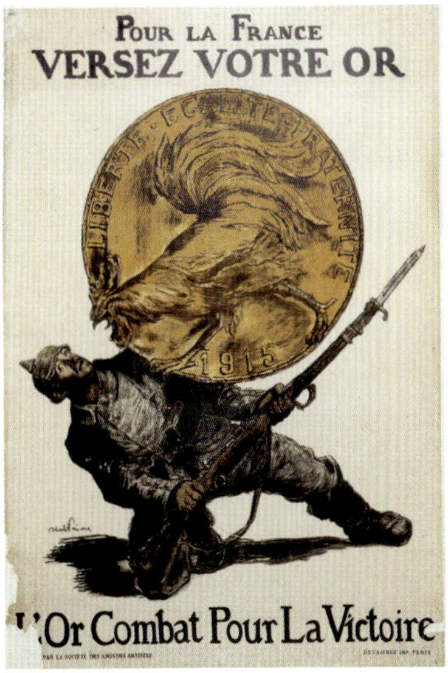

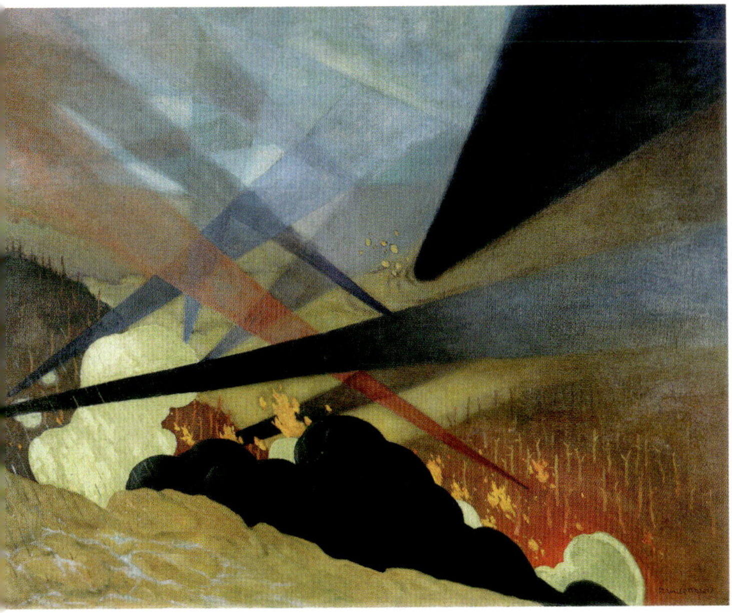

Above: Abel Faivre, *Pour la France, versez votre or. L'or combat pour la victoire, 1915*, poster.

Opposite: Félix Vallotton (1865-1925), *Verdun, interpreted war painting, black, blue and red coloured projections, devastated land, clouds of gas*, 1917, oil on canvas, 1.14 x 1.46 m.
An almost abstract composition of this devastated landscape beneath a horizon crossed by light beams reflecting the dehumanising violence of industrial war.

the Frenchman Marshal Foch Supreme Commander of the Allied Forces, the Germans retreated. An armistice was signed in France on 11 November 1918.

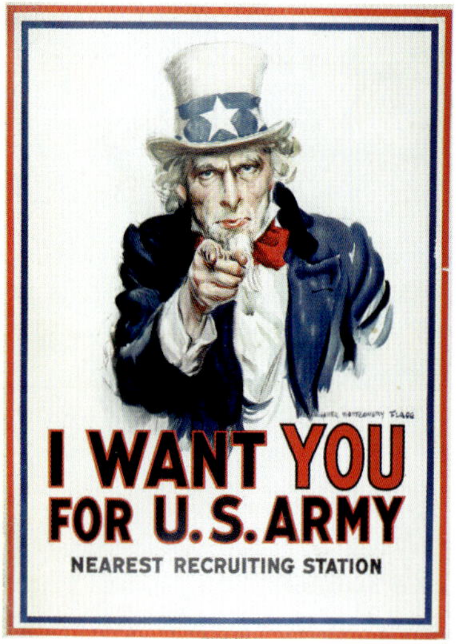

James Montgomery Flagg, I want you for the US Army, 1917, poster. For this recruitment poster with a print run of over 5 million, the illustrator depicts himself as Uncle Sam, a character symbolising the United States of America.

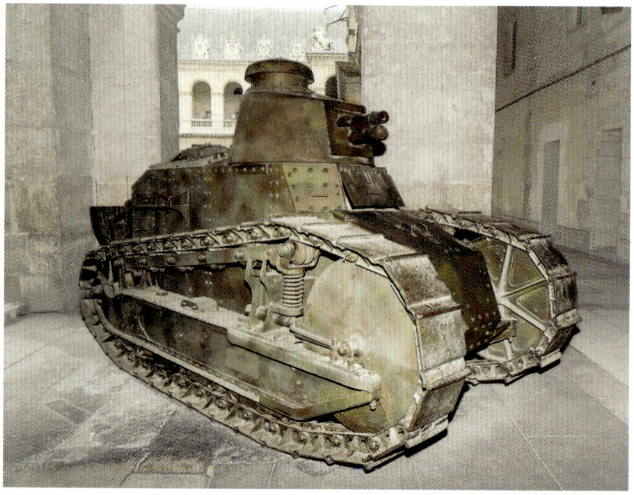

Renault FT 17 tank, France, 1917 steel, 1.74 x 2.14 m, 6.5 t.

Between the two world wars (1919-1939)

Victorious France enjoyed considerable international prestige, as evidenced by the batons of the Marshal of France, Great Britain and Poland of Ferdinand Foch. The country was, however, severely weakened by the deaths of 1.4 million men, plus 5 million wounded, often severely mutilated, as evidenced by plaster casts of "broken faces". Very present in social and political life, veterans kept the memory of all victims alive including those shot as an example.

In the post-war period, France exerted its influence in Eastern Europe and the Balkans. Globally, its outreach was founded on the Empire, which reached its peak in territorial terms. The attachment of the French to "Greater France" was illustrated at the 1931 Colonial Exhibition in Paris.

Faced with the increasing dangers embodied by Italian fascism, the Spanish Civil War and especially German Nazism, the French Army adopted a defensive strategy based on the Maginot Line, in contradiction with the alliances entered into in Eastern Europe.

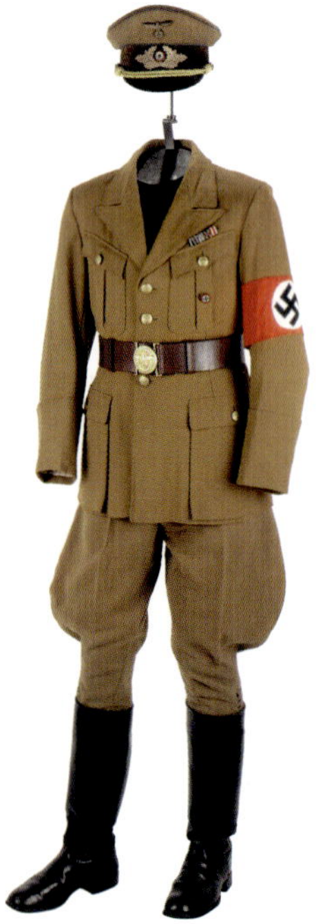

Uniform of a high-ranking member of the Nazi party in 1939. The Nazi regime militarised German society.

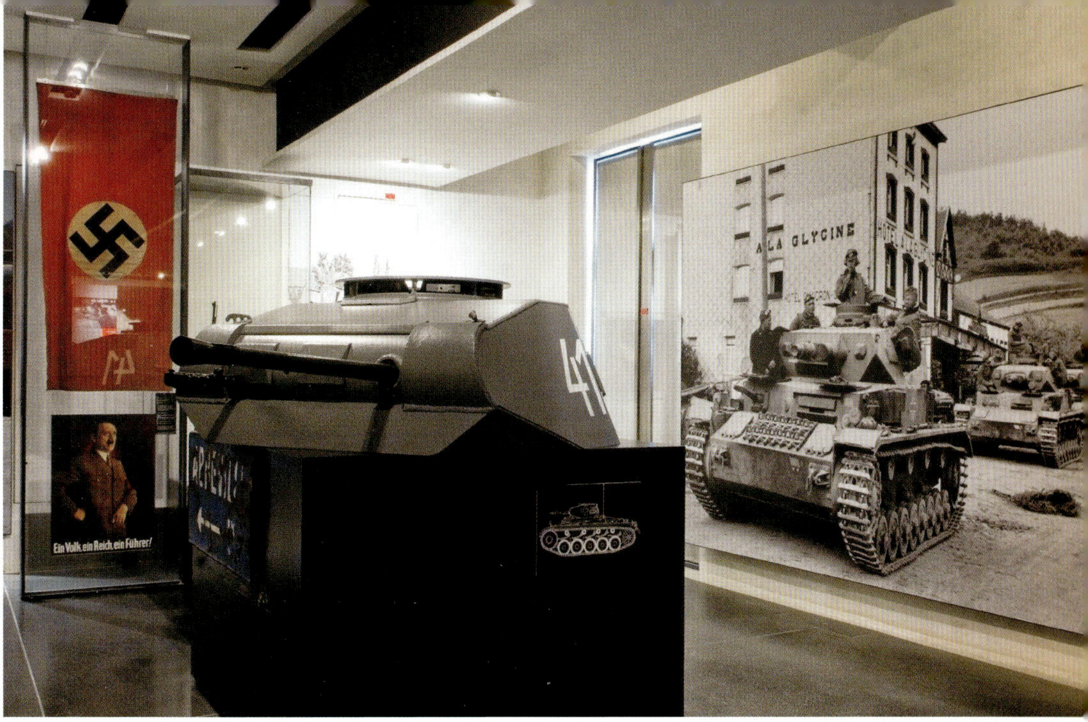

Leclerc room: Turret of German Panzer II tank used during the Battle of France (1940).

World War II (1939-1945)

The invasion of Poland by Nazi Germany brought Great Britain and France into the war on 3 September 1939.

After the wait-and-see approach of the "phoney war", the campaign in France during May-June 1940 ended in a lightening German victory resulting from the combined deployment of aircraft and tanks. Paris fell on 14 June, while more than 8 million civilians took to the roads during the exodus.

On 17 June 1940, Marshal Pétain, the new head of government, announced his intention to stop fighting. But on 18 June in London, via a broadcast on the BBC, General de Gaulle called on the French to continue the struggle and founded Free France.

The Franco-German armistice of 22 June allowed Germany to occupy the entire north and west of France. Pétain's government moved to Vichy in the unoccupied zone. The marshal became head of the French state and established an anti-republican regime, which was xenophobic and anti-Semitic. In October 1940, Pétain went down the avenue of collaboration with Hitler.

Threatened by invasion in turn, Great Britain was attacked by the Luftwaffe during the summer of 1940. With the information provided by coastal radars, the mobilisation of many women auxiliaries and the courage of its pilots, the Royal Air Force successfully defended the UK.

The conflict became global in 1941 when, on 22 June, the Soviet Union was attacked by Germany, so breaching the pact of non-aggression signed on 23 August 1939, in application of the Nazi

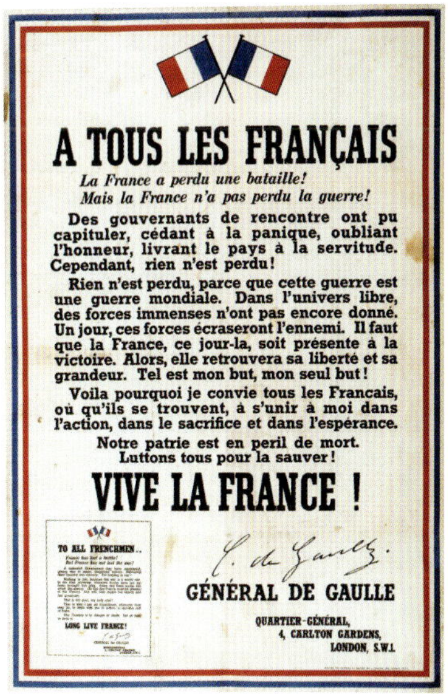

General de Gaulle's proclamation "A tous les Français" (To all the French) 1940, poster. This famous poster was created after the radio broadcast by General de Gaulle on 18 June 1940.

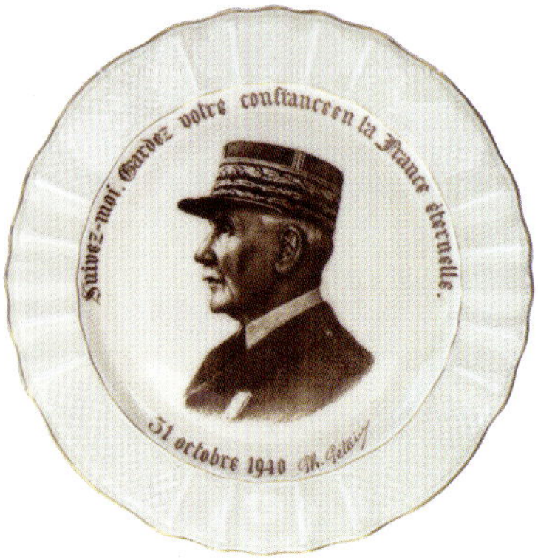

Limoges porcelain plate bearing the image of Marshal Pétain, France, 1940.

theory of "living space". After the destruction of their fleet at Pearl Harbor by Japanese forces in December 1941, the United States pledged total war against the Axis nations (Japan, Germany and Italy), particularly on the industrial level: three display cases are needed to present the entire pack of a single American soldier or GI.

From 1942 to 1943, the battles of Stalingrad, El Alamein and Guadalcanal shifted the course of the war in favour of the Allies. The sand yellow 75-mm field gun recalls the heroic resistance of the Free French at Bir Hakeim, Libya (May-June 1942). But in the European territories occupied by Germany, the oppression of civilians intensified, especially with the implementation of the Holocaust, symbolised by the introduction of the wearing of the yellow star in May 1942. In November of the same year, France was fully occupied.

Meanwhile, domestic resistance developed its intelligence, propaganda and sabotage actions. It organised the Maquis resistance and slowed the advance of the German armed forces following the Allied landings in Normandy on 6 June 1944. That of Provence, on 15 August 1944, is characterised by the large contingent from the French colonial empire using American equipment: troops from North Africa, Senegalese soldiers, etc.

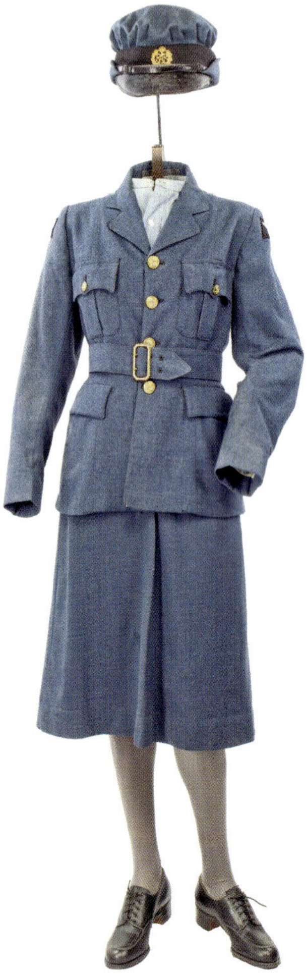

Uniform of female auxiliary in the Royal Air Force, Battle of Britain (1940).

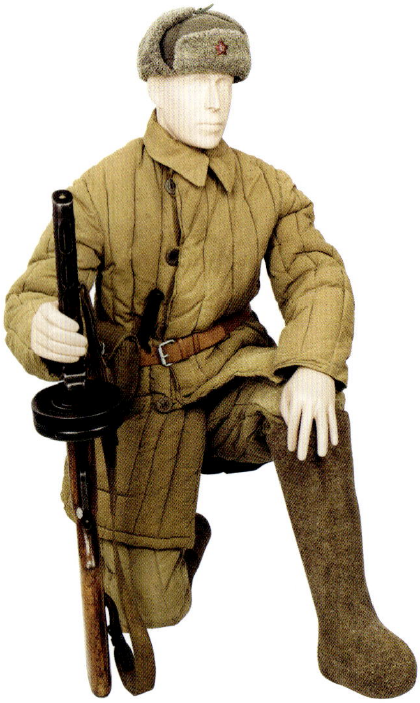

Soviet infantryman in winter uniform, 1941 model, Battle of Stalingrad (1942-1943).

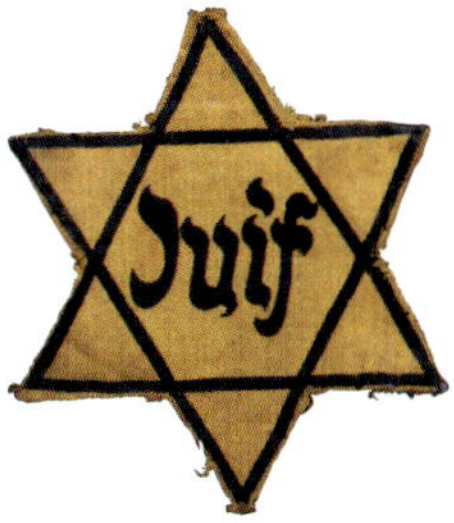

Yellow star, made compulsory for Jews from May 1942 onwards in the occupied zone.

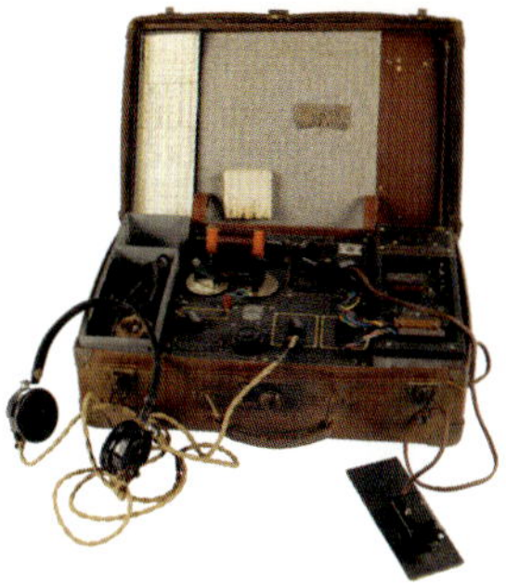

Radio transmitter-receiver used by the Resistance, circa 1943-1944.

Paris, whose population rose up against the occupier upon the call of the Resistance, was liberated on 25 August 1944 by the 2nd Armoured Division under General Leclerc. The following day, Charles de Gaulle, leader of the Provisional Government of the French Republic, triumphantly strolled down the Champs-Elysees. The Vichy regime had breathed its last.

In 1945, Germany was bombed and invaded in the west by the Americans, the British and the French, and in the east by the Soviets. The German surrender was signed in May, a few days after Hitler's suicide. Several personal items taken from his home in Berchtesgaden are exhibited.

In Germany and Poland, the Allies liberated the terrible concentration and extermination camps to which anti-Nazis, homosexuals, hostages, resistance fighters were deported ... and where Jews, Gypsies and Slavs were exterminated. The total number of Jewish victims was nearly 6 million.

In Asia, the cessation of hostilities followed the dropping of two American atomic bombs on the Japanese cities of Hiroshima and Nagasaki on 6 and 9 August 1945.

With more than 50 million dead, of which 30 million civilians, the Second World War was the deadliest conflict in human history.

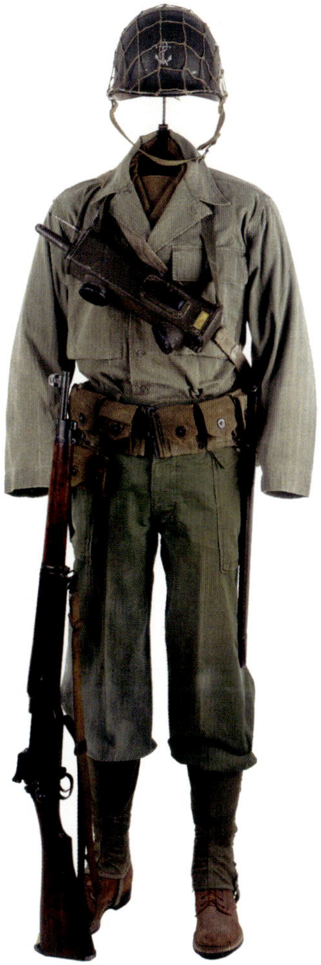

Senegalese soldier uniform, landing in Provence (1944).

Life-size model of the "Little Boy" atomic bomb dropped on Hiroshima on 6 August 1945.

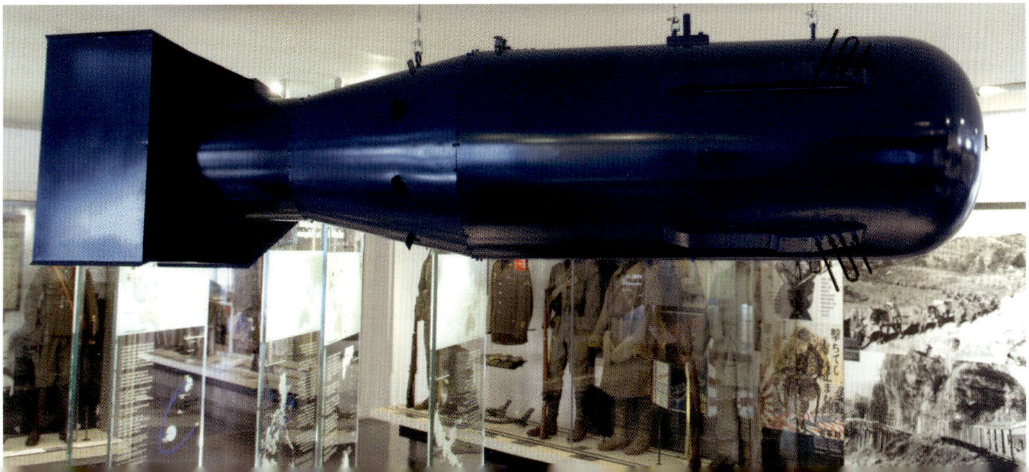

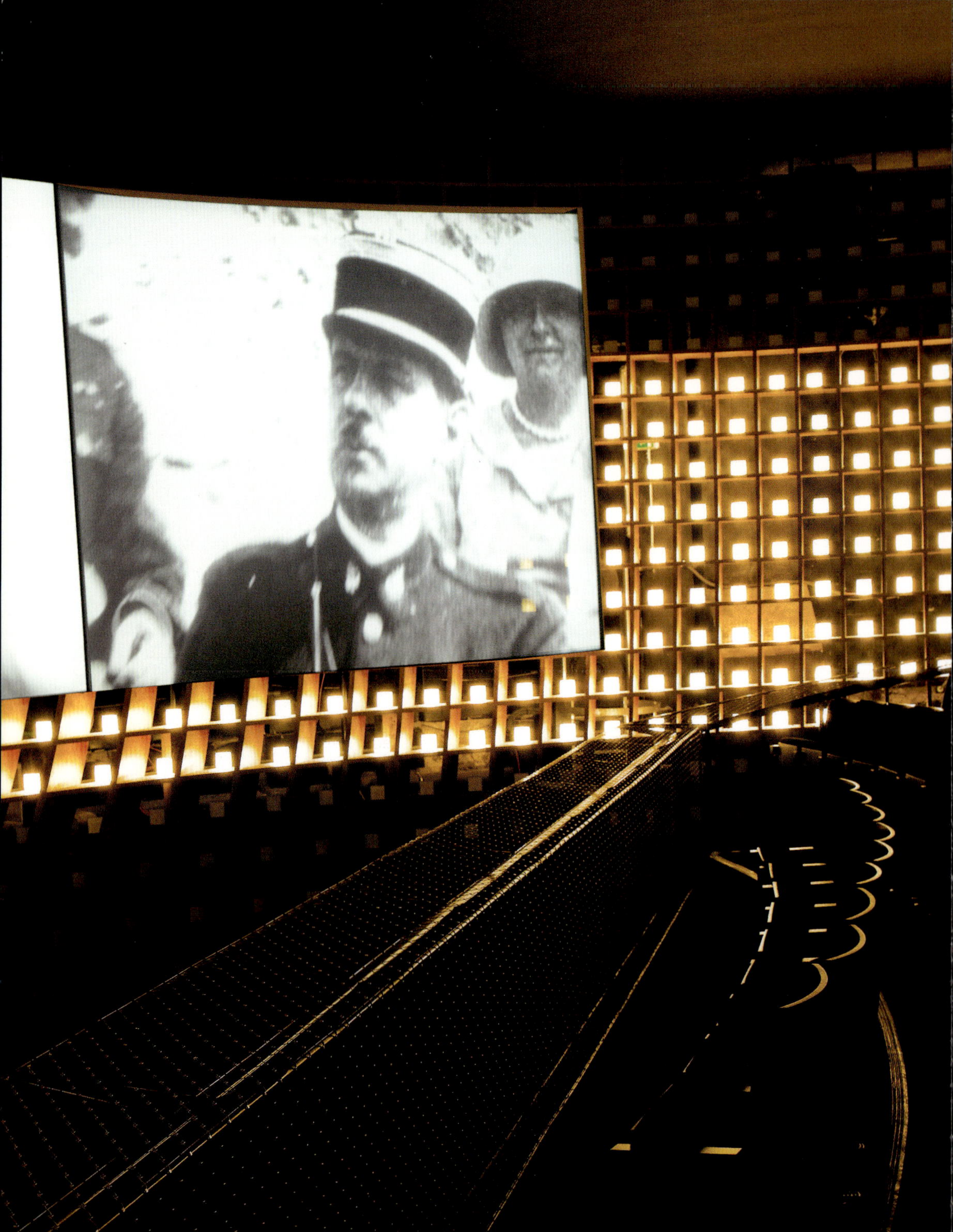

The Charles de Gaulle monument

Opened in 2008, the Charles de Gaulle monument is a joint creation of the Army Museum and the Charles de Gaulle Foundation. Designed by architects Moatti and Rivière, this area covering 2,500 square metres is dedicated to the life and public actions of General de Gaulle (1890-1970), a major figure in the history of France and the 20th century. A place of learning based on image and sound, the Monument gives visitors a chance to access a wide variety of multimedia. The tour comprises two stages: the biographical film and the interactive circuit.

The biographical film

The heart of the Monument, the multi-screen room shaped like an inverted dome, is a reference to Les Invalides where Napoleon I rests. It has five large screens with a total surface area of 60 square metres, on which the film *Charles de Gaulle, a biography* is projected. Produced by the Charles de Gaulle Foundation with the patronage of the "Les Gueules cassées" association, this film offers an initial encounter with "the man of 18 June 1940", particularly for the many foreign visitors to Les Invalides. Lasting 25 minutes, it is repeatedly broadcast every 30 minutes, with versions available in eight languages: French, English, German, Italian, Spanish, Russian, Chinese and Japanese. Directed by Olivier Brunet from archive footage, it brings to life the exceptional destiny of Charles de Gaulle through a series of six tableaus built around key dates in the General's life: 1890, 1940, 1944, 1958, 1968 and 1970. The commentary, read by Francis Huster, was written by the resistance fighter, writer and French academy member Maurice Druon (1918-2009). The music was composed by Bruno Coulais.

Discover Charles de Gaulle at Les Invalides

On the site of Les Invalides, General de Gaulle is evoked in three different places accessible to the public:
- The rooms of the Army Museum devoted to the two World Wars displays objects relating to the life of De Gaulle before 1940, to the call of 18 June, the Free French Forces, the Resistance, the Liberation and the Allied victory in 1945.
- The Museum of the Order of the Liberation: located in the western part of the Hôtel, this museum hosts collections related to the Companions of the Liberation, a title given to individual and collective members of the Order of the Liberation, a distinction created by General de Gaulle in 1940. Topics include Free France, the Resistance and Deportation.
- The Charles de Gaulle Monument presented here.

Screening of the film *Charles de Gaulle, a biography* in the multi-screen room of the Monument.

The interactive tour

The exit of the multi-screen room opens on to the " march of the century", a glass ring with a visual timeline of the history of the 20th century through until 1970.
This wall of images links up the entrance "doors" of the three rooms of the permanent exhibition, featuring various multimedia equipment: interactive book, dynamic walls, animated maps, filmed contributions from historians, touchscreens.
In the first room, the public discovers the route taken by "the man of 18 June" between 1890 and 1943. The space presents his youth, his studies at Saint-Cyr, his experience of the Great War and his official activities to which were added those of the writer and military theorist. The campaign of France in 1940, the call of 18 June, the establishment of Free France and the unification of the Resistance complete this part of the tour.
The second room, called "The Liberator", is set in the context of the liberation of the country and of Algiers, the capital of Free France, in Paris. Head of the provisional government, De Gaulle restored republican liberties, organised the punishment of collaborators, had important reforms adopted (nationalisations, voting rights for women, creation of social security, etc.) and started rebuilding the country. He resigned on 20 January 1946.
The "wilderness years", during which he wrote his *War Memoirs*, ended in 1958, the date on which the third room opens around

Use of an animated book to present works written by Charles de Gaulle before 1940.

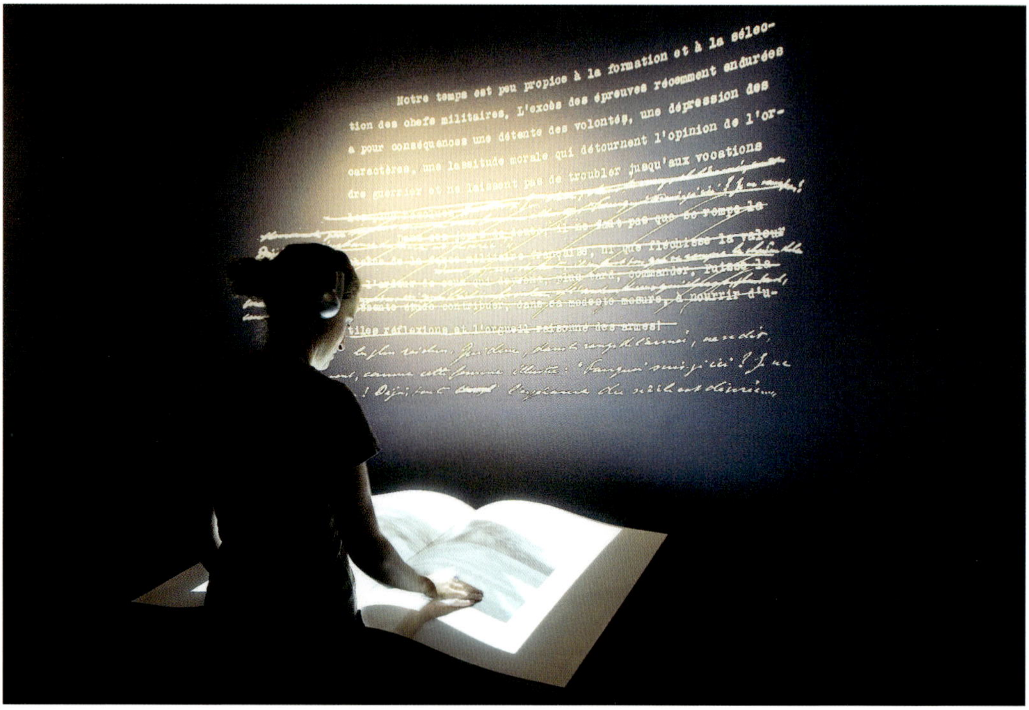

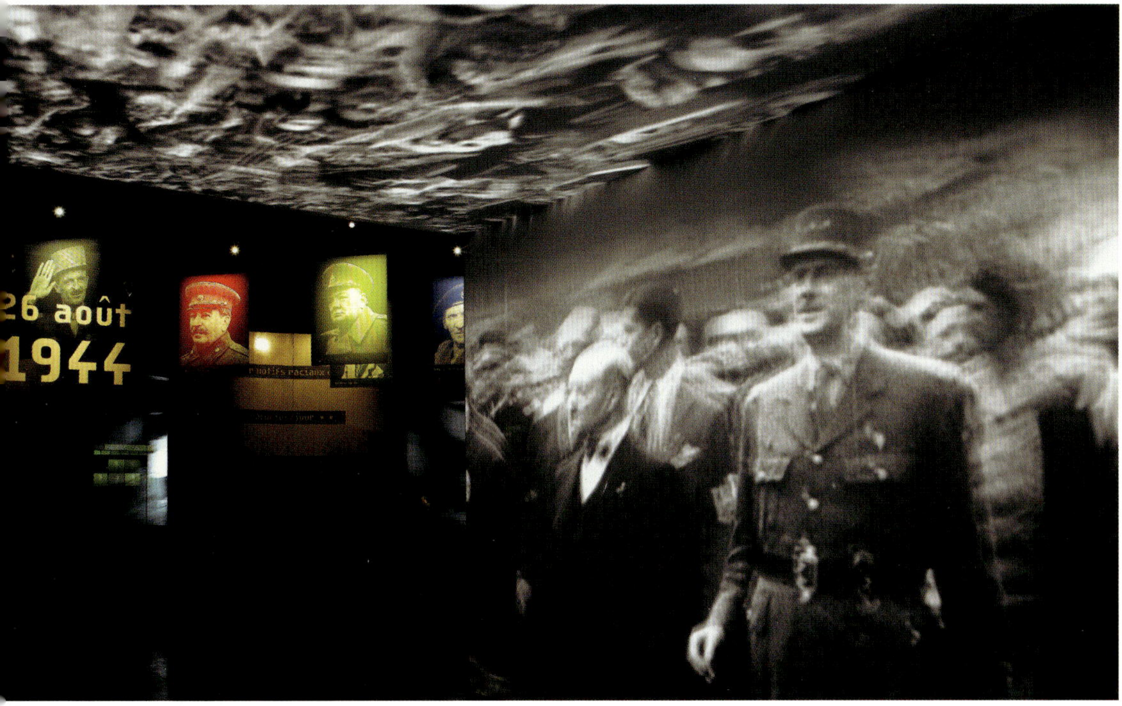

the theme of the foundation and the beginning of the Fifth Republic. Returned to power during the war in Algeria, the general was elected President of the Republic and significantly strengthened the powers of this function. In terms of foreign affairs, he completed the decolonisation process and oversaw a policy of national independence. But the 1968 protests weakened the regime. In 1969, Charles de Gaulle retired from political life and died in 1970.

Door of the "Liberator" room. On the right, walk down the Champs Elysees by General de Gaulle in liberated Paris on 26 August 1944.

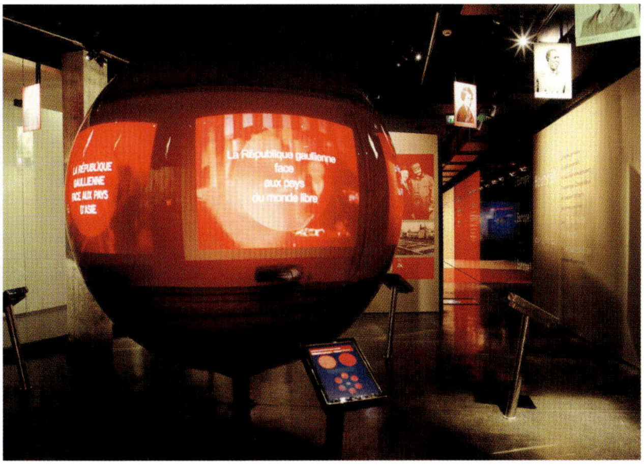

Interactive globe presenting the foreign policy of President de Gaulle in the 1960s.

The documentary centre and iconographic collections

Located in the West Wing of the Invalides, the documentary centre and the room of graphic and photographic arts of the Army Museum provides access to iconographic collections, as well as books from the library.

Displayed or kept in reserve, iconographic collections form a remarkable ensemble of 2,300 paintings, 800 sculptures, 6,100 drawings, 20,000 prints and 50,000 photographs. The history of the Hôtel des Invalides since its foundation but also the military history of France, from the Wars of Religion until today, are among the main themes of this collection.

The library of the Army Museum offers readers access to extensive literature in the field of arms, armour, artillery, uniforms – both French and foreign - and emblems, etc. The Hôtel des Invalides, Napoleonic history and wider military history are other major centres of interest. The 40,000 documents and 600 periodical titles, are supplemented by old and rare works such as collections and illustrated treatises.

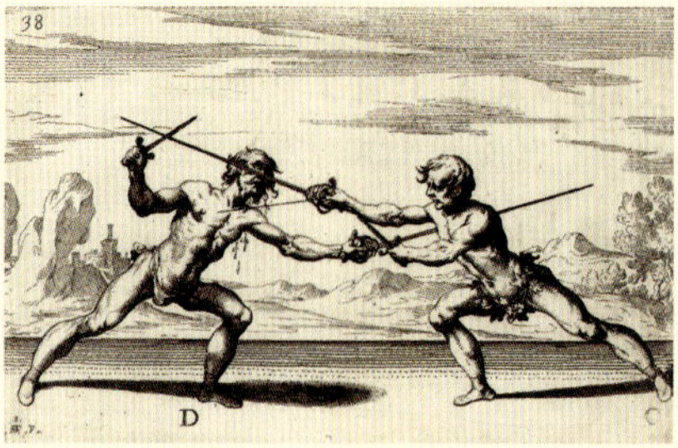

Ridolfo Capo Ferro da Cagli, *Great Treatise on the art of fencing*, Siena, 1610 etching.

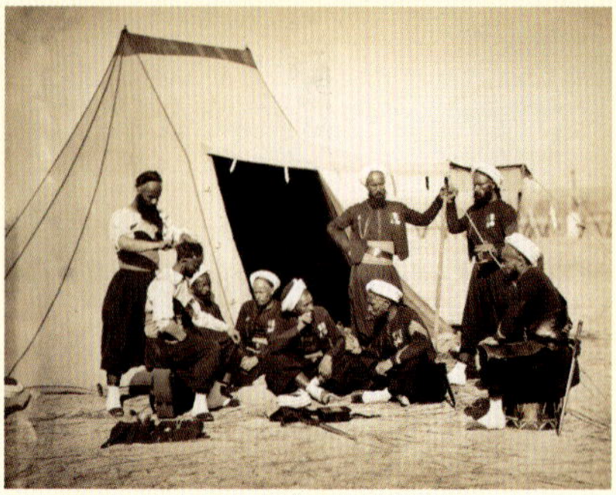

Gustave Le Gray (1820-1884), *Camp de Châlons: la toilette des zouaves*, 1857 print on albumen paper from a glass negative.

Éditions Artlys

Editorial control: Séverine Cuzin-Schulte

Publishing: Emmanuelle Maffesoli

Proofreadin: Emmanuelle Graffin

Graphics: Hervé Delemotte

Fabrication : Pierre Kegels

Photoengraving: Blackscann

Printing: Édicolor

Colophon in Cesson-Sévigné 4 december 2014

Legal deposit: January 2015

ISBN: 978-2-85495-586-6

Photographic credits

Photo © Yann Arthus-Bertrand / Altitude: p. 20; Photo © Paris, musée de l'Armée / Emilie Cambier: p. 18 (top), 19 (top), 62 / Christophe Chavan: p. 18 (bottom) / Anne-Sylvaine Marre-Noël: p. 19 (bottom) / Pascal Segrette: inside flap, p. 4, 59 (bottom); Photo © Paris - Musée de l'Armée, Dist. RMN-Grand Palais / musée de l'Armée image: p. 26 (top left), 32 (top), 45 (top), 46, 47 (top left), 49 (bottom left), 53, 54 (top left), 56 (bottom), 58 (top), 59 (top left and right), 64 (top); Photo © Paris - Musée de l'Armée, Dist. RMN-Grand Palais / Alain Argentin: p. 27 (top and bottom) / Achim Bednorz: p. 22, 25 / Marie Bruggeman: p. 13 (bottom left and right), 15 (bottom), 31 (top), 47 (top right), 48 (bottom), 59 (top centre) / Emilie Cambier: cover (bottom), back cover (top centre, bottom centre and right), p. 11 (bottom), 17, 23 (bottom centre), 24 (bottom), 26 (bottom), 29, 30 (bottom), 31 (bottom), 37 (bottom), 38 (bottom), 39 (top and bottom), 40 (right), 41 (top and bottom left), 42 (bottom), 48 (top), 49 (bottom right), 52, 55 (top right), 56 (top left and right), 58 (bottom right) / Emilie Cambier / Fanny Reynaud: p. 37 (right) / Emilie Cambier / Pascal Segrette: p. 14, 41 (bottom right) / Emilie Cambier / Tony Querrec: p. 58 (bottom left) / Christophe Chavan: p. 32, 40 (bottom left), 44, 50 (left) / Jean-Pierre Delagarde: p. 42 (top) / Jean-Yves and Nicolas Dubois: p. 43 (bottom) / Hubert Josse: p. 10 / Anne-Sylvaine Marre-Noël: back cover (top right), p. 8, 12 (top and bottom), 13 (top), 21, 23 (top, bottom left and right), 24 (top), 30 (top), 33 (top and bottom left), 34-35, 36 / Pierre Mérat: p. 51 (centre) / Christian Moutarde: cover (top), p. 6-7, 49 (top), 50 (bottom), 54 (bottom), 64 (bottom) / Tony Querrec: p. 38 (centre), 43 (left and top right and centre), 57 (top) / Caroline Rose: p. 28, 33 (bottom centre) / Pascal Segrette: back cover (top left and bottom left), p. 9, 11 (top), 15 (top), 16 (top), 33 (bottom right), 38 (top), 40 (centre left), 45 (bottom), 46 (bottom left), 47 (bottom right), 51 (left and right), 55 (top left, bottom left and right), 54 (top), 60, 63 (top and bottom) / Sebastian Sraessle: p. 40 (top); Photo © RMN-Grand Palais / Jean-Gilles Berizzi: p. 16, 59 (bottom).